RIVER & COASTAL WALKS IN ESSEX

Mel Birch

a
CASTELL
publication

RICHARD CASTELL PUBLISHING LIMITED

ISBN 0 948134 43 7

First Published July 1997 by
RICHARD CASTELL PUBLISHING LIMITED
Thwaite, Eye, Suffolk IP23 7EE

Text © 1997 Mel Birch

Printed by
THE GIPPING PRESS
Lion Barn Industrial Estate, Needham Market, Suffolk IP6 8NZ

CONTENTS

INTRODUCTION

IN THIS THE SECOND of the series on river and coastal walks in East Anglia, we explore the coast and waterways of Essex in twenty-three fascinating walks covering all but the southern, London fringe, of the county.

The Essex border is four-fifths water - Stour in the north, sea on the east, Thames on the south and Lea and Stort to the west, and while the scenery is nowhere spectacular, its tranquil beauty has a considerable attraction. The charming wooded and abundant hedgerows, and undulating and well-wooded hills alternate with highly cultivated land and pasture dotted with picturesque villages and hamlets intersected with winding lanes. The landscape echoes neighbouring Suffolk, especially in the north-east corner where the Stour's pastoral beauty is shared by both counties and reflected in some of John Constable's greatest works.

However, it is in the areas of mudflats, 'saltings' and other marshy lands which fringe the southern and eastern coast lines, and the islands of Mersea, Foulness, Wallasea and the smaller Bridgemarsh, Osea, Northey, Horsey, etc. - usually considered the least interesting to the casual observer - that the county inherits its own particular character. These areas, rich in natural history, possess a fascinating mystical atmosphere, particularly at sunrise and sunset.

The rivers featured in this edition are: the Stour, about 50 miles long and formed from three Suffolk tributaries. It becomes navigable at Ballingdon near Sudbury, widens out into a considerable estuary at Manningtree, and enters the North Sea off Harwich. The Colne is 35 miles long, rising on the northern border near Birdbrook. It is navigable from Colchester where it turns almost due south and is joined by the Roman River opposite Wivenhoe to reach the sea between Brightlingsea and Mersea Island. Bourne Brook meanders through the county for 17 miles to reach the Thames at Dagenham. The Pant rises in Wimbush and runs for 33 miles, changing its name to Blackwater on the way at Bocking. The Chelmer rises in Debden, is 50 miles long, and was made navigable from Chelmsford. It joins the Blackwater estuary near Maldon to reach the sea. The Crouch is 35 miles long and navigable from Hull Bridge to the sea. The Stort, which forms the boundary with Hertfordshire rises on the Essex border and flows 48 miles to the Thames. For over half this distance it is joined by the River Lea. The river was canalised from Bishop Stortford in 1769 to form the Lea & Stort Navigation. The unpretentious Roding rises in Easton Park near Dunmow and flows for about 40 miles to join the Thames at Barking Creek.

Other rivers not walked in this book include the Lea, which enters Essex near Roydon and flows into the Thames west of Victoria Docks, and the Rouch, a cofluent of the Crouch which joins near its mouth by a channel between the islands of Wallasea and Foulness.

Further north the coast is indented by Walton Creek and Hamford Water which, after surrounding a group of islands, runs some miles inland.

4

The marine flora of Essex is extensive. On the stretches of shingle and sand bordering the sea you will find horned poppy, sea rocket, sea kale and saltwort together with various species of orache and sea spurge. On the 'saltings', golden and marsh samphires thrive along with thrift, sea lavenders, sea aster, sea blite and scurvy grass; whilst waste ground and banks near the sea are home to pepperworts, sea campion, sea lettuce, asparagus, sea wormwood, wild celery and sea holly.

The extensive 'saltings', covered only occasionally by the highest tide, the considerable mudflats, left uncovered at low tide, and the grass-covered marshes recovered from the sea, form favourable feeding and breeding grounds for waders and wildfowl. Brent geese are again returning in large numbers during winter and black-headed (peewit) gulls, oystercatchers (which nest on the shingle banks), and ringed

MAP OF ESSEX SHOWING STARTING POINTS

1. Bradfield	9. Finchingfield	17. Little Baddow
2. Ramsey	10. Radwinter	18. Woodham Walter
3. Kirby le Soken	11. Coggeshall Hamlet	19. South Woodham Ferrers
4. Eight Ash Green	12. Tollesbury	20. Burnham on Crouch
5. Earls Colne	13. Mundon	21. Canewdon
6. Wivenhoe	14. Bradwell on Sea	22. Ongar
7. Brightlingsea	15. Thaxtead	23. Little Hallingbury
8. St Osyth	16. Felstead	

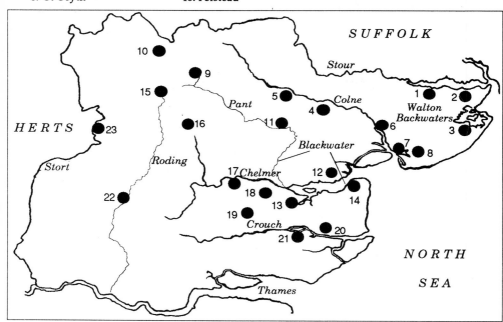

plover are popular visitors. Another inhabitant making a welcome return is the otter, now found from time to time in most Essex rivers and reed-beds, and in dykes on the marshes.

Several of the major rivers have strong historic association. The defensive topography of the Colne and Roman River made an attractive settlement area for early invaders culminating in its occupation by the Romans who founded Camulodunum here (present-day Colchester). The Battle of Maldon between Earl Brihtnoth and the invading Danes took place on the banks of the Blackwater in 991 and The Battle of Ashingdon, between Edmund Ironside and the Danes under Cnut (Canute), on the hills above the Crouch in 1016.

Many of the old industries which once traded on or beside the rivers and estuaries have long since gone leaving tantalising glimpses of rusting machinery, derelict or converted tide mills or the earthwork banks of long dismantled railway tracks. Some remain, though often in contracted form, notably oyster rearing along the estuaries and creeks of the Blackwater, Crouch, Rouch and, particularly, the Colne where it has been a major industry since pre-Roman times. These grounds appear to be the natural home of the native oyster owing to the particular character of the water and more especially the sheltered position of the river-beds where an equable temperature is maintained at the critical time of spawning (or spatting). Another important industry of the sea-coast is that of yacht building though, again, much of the trade has been lost, this time to the north through the change in construction from wood to steel and aluminium.

Enjoy the walks, but remember always to;

FOLLOW THE COUNTRY CODE

Leave livestock, crops and machinery alone.
Take your litter home.
Help to keep all water clean.
Protect wildlife, plants and trees.
Take special care on country roads.
Make no unnecessary noise.
Enjoy the countryside and respect its life and work.
Guard against all risk of fire.
Fasten all gates.
Keep your dogs under close control.
Keep to public paths across farmland.
Use gates and stiles to cross fences, hedges and walls.

The River Stour

For Stour, a daintie flood, that duly doth divide
Fair Suffolke from this shire upon her other side,
By Clare first coming in, and Sudbury doth show,
The even course she keepes; when farre she doth not flow,
But Breton a bright nymph, fresh succour to her brings:
Yet is she not so proud of her superfluous springs,
But Orwell coming in from Ipswitch thinkes that shee,
Should stand for it with Stour, and lastly they agree,
That since the Britans hence their first discoveries made,
And that into the east they first were taught to trade.
Besides, of all the roads, and havens of the east,
This harbour where they meet, is reckoned for the best.

(Michael Drayton)

IMMORTALISED by those two great Suffolk painters, John Constable and Thomas Gainsborough, the Stour formed the ancient division between the Kingdom of East Anglia and the County of Essex.

Although its source is in Cambridgeshire all its three tributaries, the Glem, the Box and the Brett, rise in Suffolk.

It is a large river, being over one mile wide in places and fifty miles long, but the last ten, being tidal, leave only a narrow channel below Wrabness to Mistley at low tide.

Its only town on the Essex bank is Manningtree which trades in milling, malting and timber, but the port of Harwich forming East Anglia's gateway to the Continent, stands at the Orwell-Stour Estuary.

Wool was the greatest factor in the prosperity of the towns and villages which border the Stour, but this great East Anglian industry gradually declined through the latter half of the 16th century, and little has come since to replace it.

In the reign of Queen Anne an Act of Parliament in 1705 allowed for making the river navigable from Manningtree to Sudbury on the Suffolk side; the work started in 1708 and took five years. However, the trade it created was later lost to the railways.

The Stour at Wrabness (Walk 1).

RIVER STOUR
Walk 1: Bradfield to Wrabness

Start:	*Take the B1352 from Manningtree and at Bradfield leave it by carrying straight on towards Wix. Park a short distance along this road in the Community Centre car park on the left.*
O.S.Maps:	*Landranger 169; Pathfinder 1053 & 1078.*
Distance:	*9½ miles.*
Refreshments:	*Strangers Home & The Village Maid, Bradfield and pub in Wrabness.*
Description:	*The main feature of this walk is the 3 mile stretch of the lovely river Stour, here at its widest and most impressive. There is a price to pay, however, in the form of the long and rather arduous length of field walking which forms part of the section which turns this into a circular walk.*

LEAVE THE COMMUNITY CENTRE car park and turn left. Cross over the road junction passing The Village Maid public house into Heath Road. Turn left into Dairy House Lane, a 'No Through Road'.

Beyond the houses the lane heads down between high hedges. At Bluehouse Farm turn left between the buildings passing the farmhouse on your right and head down a grass track bearing right and left to follow the right side of a hedge with a field on your right. At the end of the field follow the boundary right with a ditch on your left. Carry on, ignoring a plank bridge and footpath sign going left. At the end of the field cross the ditch in front of you and head through the trees. Cross another ditch to come out at the edge of a cultivated field where you turn right and left to follow the boundary. As you climb you pass an attractive area of water on your right enclosed by large banks, presumably artificially created for irrigation purposes. Continue on now along the right side of a narrow field with another larger lake edged with willows on the right.

Beyond this you climb to go through an opening to reach a farm track. Carry straight on along this and when it turns left go with it for a few steps then leave it to turn right and continue in the same direction as before along the right side of the field. When level with the end of a row of trees bordering the farm buildings, turn left and cross straight over this narrow field, picking up a short length of track before entering the farmyard. Carry on through to meet a country lane.

Turn right for a few yards before turning left at the footpath sign to head straight over a large cultivated field keeping the line of telegraph poles over on your right. On the far side you should locate a footpath sign. Cross a plank bridge and ditch and continue on across the next field. Go over a culvert here into a lane and turn right.

Follow the lane as it bends left by Willow Hall Cottage and reach the Hall itself. The lane becomes a track and you fork right, heading past outbuildings to reach a rough area of grass beyond. Turn left and walk to the end of the field and turn right following a track along the left side of the field passing a single oak tree. Continue on along the side of a meadow with an open field on the right, then with a ditch on your left. Ignore the first plank bridge and waymarker pointing left, but shortly after, confronted by a small copse, take the second one left. Turn right and then left to follow the field boundary to meet a track.

Turn right towards Butlers Farm and left to follow the boundary fence. At the end continue ahead, straight over the field. At the end continue over the next heading for the right corner where you cross a stream over a wide culvert and carry on as before along the left side of the field on your right to reach the road on an S bend. Cross the road and the plank bridge on the far side to continue along the field edge. Cross straight over a farm track and continue along the right side of a cultivated field, later with a hedge on your right, to reach the road at Wrabness. Cross the road in front of the row of houses. (Your route is right but you may wish to take a short detour left for refreshments at the pub if it is open).

Turn right and walk past the houses. Immediately past Hill Crest take the wide track left and head down to the railway bridge. (You can shorten your walk by crossing it and heading down the well-worn path between open fields to the river but in doing so you will miss a pleasant woodland walk). The main route turns right along another well-used path, again between open fields, passing a pond on your right. Cross stiles and enter the ancient Stour Wood managed by the RSPB. Walk through the trees and cross over a track. A few yards on you reach another and this time you turn left. The track bends right and you follow it running parallel

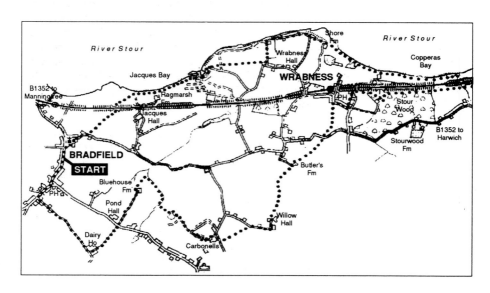

10

with the railway embankment. **When it divides keep on ahead down to a footbridge and up the far side. Cross another footbridge and continue beside the embankment. A stile leads you out along a narrow path fenced from a meadow on your right. Reach Copperas Wood, another nature reserve, and turn left to cross the railway bridge. Take a stile beside the gate on the left and take the path forking left. When the path divides again, fork right, then left. Cross a footbridge and head through the trees, bearing right down to Copperas Bay and another footbridge.**

The Bay takes its name from Copperas (bisulphate of iron), a material looking similar to small pieces of twig, which was dredged from the mud here and taken to Harwich to be used in the manufacture of inks and dyes. This is also an important site for wading birds and wildfowl during the winter months. From public bird-hides you can look for black-tailed godwits, dunlin, red shank, pintail, brent geese, shelduck and grey plover.

Cross the footbridge and set off along the field edge with Stour Wood over on your left. You reach an area of mudflats and saltmarsh.

This is Balhaven, an area of saltmarsh designated a site of Special Scientific Interest and in the care of English Nature. It provides a habitat for sea purslane, sea blite, sea arrowgrass, scurvy grass, sea wormwood, thrift, lesser sea spurrey and sea aster.

The length of river at Stone Point is privately owned and managed by an association of members with their own slipways and living quarters, but do not be deterred by this, ignore the footpath going left, go through the gate and continue on ahead behind the buildings. Beyond, the cliff rises dramatically above the river affording lovely views across the Holbrook Bay on the Suffolk side. You arrive at a footpath sign sending you left on a track temporarily away from the river, and this one you take. At the houses you turn right along a wide grassy track bordered by new hedging which leads you down to the impressive expanse of Jacques Bay and a little creek which unfortunately appears nameless.

Wall Lane, the little lane coming in from the left and ending at the sea wall, used to continue along the sea wall to Bradfield, emerging at the bottom of Ship Hill. It was used by light horse-drawn vehicles in the 18th and 19th century to avoid several steep hills on the inland route (now the B1352).

Climb the steps to the river bank and carry on. The area on your left looks rather strange, dotted with the remains and footings of buildings and heavy in scrub. This area is in the process of being developed as a new nature reserve.

Wrabness Nature Reserve occupies a site established as a naval mine depot in 1921 by the Ministry of Defence. It actively continued in this role until

1963 when the buildings were demolished. It then passed into Home Office control and several attempts were made to develop it. Following concerted local opposition these development proposals were finally abandoned in 1992 and the site purchased by the Wrabness Nature Reserve Charitable Trust.

Comprising 52 acres of unimproved grassland, scrub, woodland and intertidal areas of mudflats and saltmarsh, these areas provide an important habitat for a wide variety of plants, butterflies and birds.

Nightingales and warblers breed in the scrub and the unimproved grassland has a good population of butterflies and moths including cinnabar moth. The site which is a declared Local Nature Reserve (LNR), contains a rich flora, including ox-eye daisy and common centaury. Interestingly, Woolly Mammoth bones have been found nearby.

You pass Ragmarsh Farm and when level with the large impressive Jacques Hall away on your left you pick up a well-worn path heading diagonally through a field away from the river towards the railway bridge (not that in front of the hall, but the next). Pass under the railway and then continue up the field and through a meadow in the same direction to meet a short length of track in the top corner which leads you out on to the B1352.

Turn right and walk round the bend taking great care as initially there is no verge. Carry on into Bradfield and, just before the road junction where there is the first of two refreshment opportunities, the 'Stranger's Home' inn, turn left to pass through the churchyard and visit the church.

Despite the Victorian rendered exterior, St Lawrence Church is of ancient origin with a 13th century west tower, chancel, nave and font. There are also monuments to Joan Agassiz who died in 1598 and Elizabeth Agassiz, undated. In 1871, the church received a new rector in the person of Leighton G.Hayne who brought with him a monstrous church organ in ten large railway trucks. Parts of the church had to be virtually demolished to accommodate it and even more damage was caused when it was played; parts were later removed to Mistley.

After your visit carry on through the churchyard and out by the lychgate. Turn left and walk back to your starting point at the Community Centre car park, not forgetting the Village Maid, another chance to quench your thirst, just along the road.

Walton Backwaters

For while the tired waves, vainly breaking,
Seem here no painful inch to gain,
Far back, through creeks and inlets making,
Comes silent, flooding in, the main.

(Arthur Hugh Clough)

WALTON BACKWATERS is a unique area of the coast where the sea has broken in and two water courses, Hamford Water, running in a south-westerly direction and Walton Channel running south and then west to the Twizzle have cut deep channels through the shallow Pye Sand which extends from Walton on the Naze northwards to Dovercourt.

While it is open, bleak and virtually treeless this was not always so. Many local place names end in 'ley' meaning 'woodland' or 'a clearing' in woodland, evidence of a very different landscape in Saxon times.

This is a lonely, isolated place but its brooding nature creates its own special charm and the fact that the waters are almost completely land-locked makes it a popular place for light sailing.

Walton Backwaters - The old quay at Kirby-le-Soken (Walk 3)

WALTON BACKWATERS
Walk 2: Ramsey to Little Oakley

Start:	*Take the B1352 from Manningtree and turn right in Ramsey just before the roundabout at the junction with the A120. Park along the road by the Castle Inn.*
O.S.Maps:	*Landranger 169; Pathfinder 1054 & 1078*
Distance:	*6½ miles.*
Refreshments:	*Castle Inn, Ramsey.*
Description:	*The walk sets off through meadows following the course of a stream. Tracks and field paths take you to the B1414 which you must follow for a short distance before another track leads you down to Hamford Water. The river bank leads you past evocative mudflats to a coastal sand and shingle beach . Your return is along well-walked tracks partly along the Essex Way, a long-distance footpath.*

SET OFF ALONG THE STREET away from the pub and look out for a footpath sign tucked in the hedge by 'The Street' road sign. Negotiate a stile and plank bridge leading you to the A604 which you cross to another stile and plank bridge into a meadow. Cross this passing to the left of a telegraph pole to reach another stile and larger plank bridge on the far side. Continue through this meadow bearing right. Cross a stile beside a metal gate and carry on along the right side of the next meadow. Pass a farmhouse over on your right and head for the left-hand corner of the meadow where you negotiate a stile beside a farm gate. Press on along the left side of a former cultivated field now under grass following a stream bordered by mature willows. Bear left with the stream, now with a wire fence on your right and go through a wooden gate to reach a country road.

Turn left for a few yards, crossing the stream, and turn right crossing a field and passing to the right of a telegraph pole to reach a stile on the far side. Beyond the stile and plank bridge a wide grassy path leads you up the left side of a cultivated field. There are good views from the top. At the point where you come level with Great Oakley Hall over on your right you meet a track and turn left along it as it heads between open fields. You now get your first glimpse of Hamford Water away on your right. You reach the 14th century St Mary's Church tucked away in the trees and now converted to a house. The garden encompasses the churchyard, which still appears to be in use.

Turn right and walk down the drive to reach the B1414 where you turn left. There is no footpath here, so take care while you walk the short distance to Little Oakley Hall and turn right down a concrete track. The track becomes unmade and skirts an area of woodland before arriving at the river bank. Climb the bank and get your first views over Walton Backwater's moody mudflats.

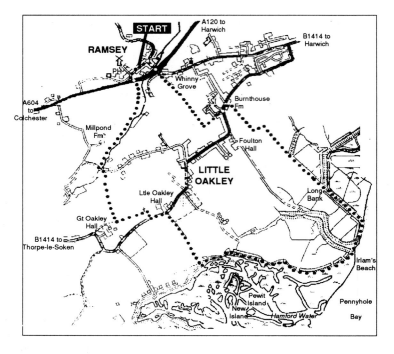

The sign barring the path to the right is hardly welcoming, threatening prosecution under the Explosives Acts of 1875 and 1923 to any trespassers.

More encouraging is the fact that the 800 hectares you will be passing by is now a Nature Reserve. It consists of intertidal mudflats supporting internationally important numbers of waders and wildfowl in winter. The most notable species are avocet, black-tailed godwit, Brent geese and teal. Wildfowl on migration in spring and autumn also use this site. The land is owned and managed by the Little Oakley and District Wildfowlers Association in conjunction with English Heritage.

Set off along the bank with Pewit Island beyond the mudflats on your right. Later you reach the open waters of Pennyhole Bay and the mudflats are replaced by a sand and shingle beach just prior to reaching the concrete wall.

Irlam's Beach has become a nesting ground for the little tern, smallest and rarest of our British terns - and even rarer in recent years. This is one of the few sites left on the British Coast.

Beyond the concrete wall the bank turns inland. When it bears right leave it to continue on straight ahead along the Essex Way, a wide track running between a ditch and a cultivated field. A well-worn path then continues between open fields and along the left side of two further fields. At the end of these, cross the ditch and turn left. Beyond the field boundary turn right and follow the right side of a cultivated field. The path skirts a grazing meadow at Burnthouse Farm to reach the road via a stile.

Cross the road and turn left. Cross Bayview Crescent and fork right along a concrete drive bordered by young trees. Pass Little Oakley Memorial Centre and walk through the car park. Beyond this pick up a well-used path heading straight on through an open field. About a third of the way across the field take another path branching off right. When you pick up the field edge the path switches to the left side of the field on the right via a plank bridge. When the hedge ends carry on ahead down the field with fine views of Ramsey with its windmill; the red-brick tower of the church is to the right. Pass to the left of Whinny Grove and come out on the road.

Cross both lanes of the road to the left of the roundabout and take the road into Ramsey beyond, crossing the bridge and bearing left at the junction back to your starting point beyond the Castle Inn. A lane on the right takes you on a short detour to visit Ramsey windmill.

> Ramsey windmill lays claim to being the most easterly windmill in Essex although it did not originate here. It was moved - reputedly by boat - to its present site in 1842 from Woodbridge in neighbouring Suffolk. It is a post-mill, the earliest of the three forms of windmill, where the main body of the mill pivots on a massive central oak post so that the sails can always face the wind.

WALTON BACKWATERS
Walk 3: Kirby Cross to Kirby-le-Soken

Start: *Take the B1035 from Manningtree. In Kirby Cross turn right to the station and park on the car park.*

O.S.Maps: *Landranger 169; Pathfinder 1078.*

Distance: *7½ miles.*

Refreshments: *Kirby Tavern and Hare & Hounds in Kirby Cross; Red Lion and The Ship in Kirby-le-Soken.*

Description: *Well-used paths take you to Kirby-le-Soken where, after a pleasant walk along the length of the street you take a track down to Hamford Water opposite Horsey Island. An easy walk along the elevated bank which snakes round the mudflats is only broken once to visit the evocative old quay. The return to Kirby Cross is a little less straightforward. A track which leads you back to the road is followed by a length of road walking and a rather vague field walk with no signs to assist you.*

WALK OUT OF STATION ROAD and turn left. Cross the street and turn right by the Jet service station as directed by the footpath sign. Walk through the forecourt and take the well-used path beyond over the grass and heading through open fields. Another path goes left but you carry on ahead over the remainder of the field. Continue on a track past the bowls club and tennis court, but at the end of the football pitch do not follow the track right but instead look for a footpath on your left going through the hedge and turning right.
Head down the open field passing under the power lines with the church at Kirby-le-Soken ahead. Pick up a grassy path along the right side of the field and then along the left side of the next field bordered by a post and rail fence. Follow the field boundary and enter the churchyard to visit St Michael's Church.

St Michael's is large and very impressive with attractive and intricate flintwork. In 1833 the building experienced considerable rebuilding which was later covered by the restorer Henry Stone.

Come out on the street and cross to the Red Lion where you turn right and follow the footpath through the attractive village of Kirby-le-Soken. Pass the War Memorial, The Ship public house and Quay Lane which leads down to the old quay (which we shall visit later). Leave the village and carry on past Turpins Lane on your right until you reach Island Lane by Brick Barn Farm on your left. Turn left here and carry on down this wide stony track bordered by hedges to reach the river wall by a pillbox.

This is the area of mudflats, islands and fingers of water known collectively as Walton Backwaters. Across the water is Horsey Island, reached by Island Road, a track submerged beneath The Wade during high tide. The channel of water coming in from the right is called The Twizzle which leads from Walton Channel. The whole area is a haven for a wide variety of waders and wildfowl.

The business of oyster rearing in the Backwaters was started by William Backhouse, who bred Arab horses on Horsey Island, but the first oysters froze to death in the severe winter of 1962. Success was achieved when the layers were restarted with wild European oysters from Cornwall.

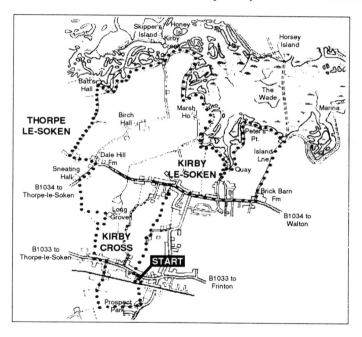

Turn left and set off along the bank. At Peter's Point the bank swings left and you head for the old Kirby Quay where you cross the footbridge. Turn left to walk along Quay Lane as far as the little black thatch-roofed cottage.

Up until the First World War there was considerable barge traffic using the quays at Kirby, Walton and Oakley, and the large warehouse built further on at Landermere Quay; a channel known as Beaumont Cut was specially dug to enable barges to reach Beaumont Quay at the very head of the Backwater.

19

Cross the ditch over on your right and turn back to pick up a well-used path along the edge of the field. It is best to continue along the field edge rather than the bank which runs parallel but is very overgrown in places. Later, at the end of the field, you turn through the hedge on your right, and after a few yards, are able to pick up the river bank again. You pass the isolated ruined buildings of Marsh House away on your left. The path later swings left and immediately right before heading straight out to a point immediately opposite Horsey Island. Round the point and Kirby Creek and the tiny Honey Island face you across the water. You reach a point where the bank bends right, passing a small building and what appears to be an air-raid shelter, with the wooded Skipper's Island over on your right housing a Nature Reserve under the Essex Wildlife Trust. The next raised wooded island is a part of Skipper's Island only linked by an almost indistinguishable causeway. At a point where you pass a group of four fir trees, the path swings left. It bends right again and a short distance after this you reach the sparse remains of Batt's Hall, now comprising little more than a few brick footings.

Leave the bank at this point and head away through the site, now dotted with newly planted trees, to pick up the wide farm track beyond. Later the track swings left and you leave it to continue ahead across an area of rough grass and light scrub. Make your way past a small pond, cross a dry ditch, and walk along the edge of a field for a few yards to pick up a green lane still continuing in the same direction as before. Eventually the lane passes the buildings of Dale Hill Farm to reach the road.

Turn left and pass Maranatha bungalow to reach the junction with the B1034. Turn right across the grass and walk along the right side of the road up the hill and cross the road just after Monks Ridge to take the track running between open fields. The track ends and you continue with a hedge on your right to the end of the field. Pass through the hedge to reach a wide grass 'ride' running beside an arable field. Turn left and walk to the end. Turn right by the hedge and walk to the field boundary which you follow right and then left to pick up a well-walked path along the left side of the field. At the end you pass along a shady path enclosed by high hedges to come out on the street in Kirby Cross.

Turn left and just before the Hare & Hounds (a possible refreshment stop) cross the road and take Chapel Lane which goes off right. At the bottom you cross the railway via two stiles. Continue ahead, passing two greenhouses on a wide grass path, then along a short length of shady green lane. Cross a stile and walk along the right side of a grazing meadow to another stile. A few yards further on you meet a cross track called Prospect Park and turn left walking between open fields towards a group of properties. Here you carry on along the footpath with the B1032 over on your right, and past the last house, turn left along a shingle drive serving two properties. Beyond this a well-worn path heads between open fields to reach the railway again. Cross via two gates beside the station to reach the car park and your starting point.

The River Colne

Hurrah for the Dredge, with its iron edge,
And its mystical triangle.
And its hided net, with meshes set
Odd fishes to entangle.
The ship may rove through the waters above
'Mid scenes exciting wonder
But braver sights the dredge delights
As it roves the waters under.

Then a dredging we will go brave boys.
Then a dredging we will go.

(E.Forbes)

THE COLNE will forever be linked with the Romans who sailed it and built their great city of Camulodunum - present-day Colchester - here on its banks. Not that they were the first to settle and trade on the river; finds from Palaeolithic, Neolithic, Bronze and Celtic periods have been made and the Romans themselves had at first utilised an earlier fortified site recognised in a series of ditches and ramparts just outside the present town.

The Colne has its source one mile south-west of Birdbrook in the parish of Steeple Bumpstead, and runs for 41 miles to reach the sea at Colne Point just south of Brightlingsea, the last nine being tidal.

The Famous annual Colchester Oyster Feast celebrates what is and has always been one of the main industries along the river. Here the Colchester Natives, or 'Pyefleets', reckoned by connoisseurs the most succulent oysters in the world, are reared. Brightlingsea also had a lucrative spratting industry.

River Colne - St Osyth Creek. (Walk 8)

THE RIVER COLNE
Walk 4: *Eight Ash Green, Fordstreet & Aldham*

Start: *Take the A604 Cambridge road off the A12 Colchester bypass. In Eight Ash Green, take the right turn just past the Post Office. Pass the pub and at the end of Fordham Heath turn left at the crossroads to reach the parking area on the left-hand side in front of the Green.*

O.S.Maps: *Landranger 168; Pathfinder 1077.*

Distance: *8½ miles.*

Refreshments: *There is a pub at Fordham Heath near the start and finish, and Mill Race Coffee Shop and The Shoulder of Mutton pub at Fordstreet.*

Description: *A fairly straightforward walk by track, meadow and field path to Aldham, returning via the hamlet of Fordstreet along the Colne Valley following the meandering course of the young River Colne.*

SET OFF BY TURNING LEFT along Heath Road for a few paces before turning right down a metalled track. At the footpath sign turn left over a stile beside a farm gate and after a short length of farm track follow the path along the left side of a cultivated field. Continue right with the boundary and then left. Keep along the left side of the field with fine views over to your right. Go over a stile and plank footbridge and continue through the next field beside a trim hedge to another stile leading into a grazing meadow. Turn half right and cross diagonally to the right-hand hedge and carry on along to cross a stile to a farm track.

Go a few steps right then cross another stile and plank to enter another grazing meadow. Walk a few yards ahead beside the hedge before turning right and heading across the meadow and over another stile into a very large pasture. Keep straight ahead to reach a pill-box by a single tree. Turn left here and walk straight down over the grass to pick up the end of a hedge line. Continue down the next section of meadow to locate a stile and plank bridge in the far hedge by the road. Your route is right along the road to reach a footpath sign at a point where Fordham Bridge crosses the River Colne. Go over the stile on your left across an area of rough grass to reach the right edge of Fiddler's Wood. Carry on along the right side of the wood to a point where a path goes right, following the edge of a cultivated field. Go over another plank bridge through the hedge at the end of the field and turn right. Follow the boundary left heading down the field and eventually leave it via a plank bridge over the ditch. Cross an area of rough grass picking up the river again. The field boundary bears left as the river swings away right and you leave it to head for the road at Fordstreet.

Turn right along the busy A604 for a few yards, passing the post office before turning left along New Road. After a short distance you turn left opposite Tile House, walking up the drive and bearing left to skirt the buildings by a line of fir trees. Turn right and head up a grassy path between open fields passing a pill-box. Then along the left side of a cultivated field with good views back down the valley, and across to the spectacular railway viaduct at Chappel. At the cross-track turn right heading down hill. At the bottom walk along the track to reach New Road again. Head up the wide drive opposite towards Bourchier's Hall. Pass to the right of a large building then over a stile beside white gates and a transformer. Carry on to pick up a metalled drive bordered by hedges and post and rail fencing. You leave the drive to carry on along a wide grass path bordered by a paddock with post and rail fencing on your right and a hedge on the left. When this ends you pass round metal railings and through a hedge to enter a large meadow. Continue beside an old high hedge. When this ends carry on along the right side of the meadow with a cultivated field on your right to reach Tey Road.

Turn right along this quiet country lane for a short distance before leaving it at a T-junction to take the track right, heading for Hoe Wood. Your route is to skirt its right side (the wood is under the Woodland Trust and gives access to the public but, unfortunately, you have little time to linger). When the wood ends carry straight on down the right side of the field. Pass Wick Farm and at the bottom turn left by the pond and continue on a wide track passing Wick Grove. Carry on up the far side and at the top of the meadow leave the track to turn right on to a fainter grassy track. Follow the hedge left and at the end of the field on your right turn right with the boundary to reach a stile and footbridge down the bank and in the trees on your left. Turn half right and head up and then down the large meadow, making for the brick bridge spanning the Colne.

Turn right here and set off along the river bank, crossing a footbridge and stile at the end of the meadow. Continue following the field boundary for some way until you enter the riverside garden of Mill Race Coffee Shop by a pill-box where you can obtain refreshments. Carry on over a footbridge and past a line of fir trees. Go over another footbridge before passing between a hedge and railings on your left

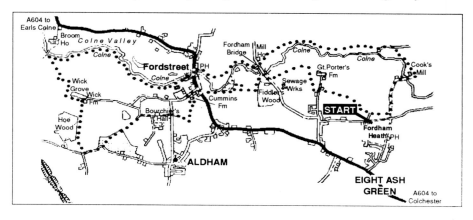

and a brick wall on the right to reach the road at Fordstreet by the entrance to Bridge House. Turn left and cross Fordstreet Bridge. Cross the road to the Shoulder of Mutton public house and head down the right side across the shingle car park to pick up the left bank of the river. The river arcs right and you carry straight on along the path heading between open fields. Pick up the river and field edge again, passing under power lines, and carry on to reach Mill Road.

Cross straight over, passing to the right of Mill House - there was a corn mill here until 1903 - and carry on along what is part of 'Essex Way', the county's long-distance footpath. Later the path leads over a footbridge and heads through a section of light woodland, over a stile and then along the left side of a long meadow. Go over a metal gate and continue with the hedge on your right. When this ends keep on ahead to pick up a farm track which leads through the next field, crossing a water course bridged by a concrete culvert. Pass a ruined brick barn and go over a stile beside a metal gate. Carry on along a wide farm track bordered by hedges. After a short distance look for a stile set in the hedge on the right. Cross this and head along the left side of the meadow to reach the Colne again. Turn left, go over a stile and follow the river bank along the right side of a cultivated field. Skirt the grounds of Cook's Mill - the fulling mill here was burnt down in 1873 - and go right, round a white gate to cross the shingle forecourt of the house. Walk along the metalled lane, crossing the river by a road bridge with the interesting sign 'Slow - small children & other animals'! Head through the avenue of trees and follow the lane left by a cottage. After another 500 yards or so, and just past the first entrance to the wood on your right, take the second over a small culvert.

The little wood is criss-crossed with paths but you keep straight ahead to reach the metalled track on which you set out. Turn left and walk back to the road at Fordham Heath and your starting point.

THE RIVER COLNE & BOURNE BROOK
Walk 5: Earls Colne to Greenstead Green

Start:	*Earls Colne is on the A604 Cambridge road from Colchester, about 4 miles from Halstead. Turn along Park Road by the church and park just beyond the school in the area of Ashwells Meadow.*
O.S.Maps:	*Landranger 168; Pathfinder 1076.*
Distance:	*9 miles*
Refreshments:	*There are restaurants and pubs in Earls Colne and a pub within 200 yards of the walk at Greenstead Green, but as this is quite a long walk it would be advisable to travel prepared.*
Description:	*The early part of the walk takes you across fields by field path, track and coutry lane to Bourne Brook. The second section follows the course of the Brook through meadows, regularly switching banks, to meet the river Colne. The third follows the course of the Colne, partly along a disused railway embankment, and the final part takes a more disjointed route past Chalkney Mill and Wood, and through fields and meadows with less than adequate signposting back via the site of the old priory to Earls Colne.*

GO THROUGH A GAP beside the wooden fence and footpath sign to the right of the school and take the concrete path heading down the valley. Fork right through a small, rough meadow and then fork right again over a stile and along an old meadow. Just before the end of the meadow the path divides, the right path heading for a wooden gate and the left to a kissing gate; take the latter. Turn left on the well-worn cross-path for a few yards by a stream to reach a cultivated field. Turn right and then follow the boundary left and right to reach the end of the field. Cross a shallow ditch to another well-walked path where you turn left. Walk up to the end of the field, going right and left at the end to come out on Curds Road on a bend.

Carry straight on for 500 yards before turning off right over a culvert and along the left side of a field. At the end cross a plank bridge and walk the right side of the next field beside an old hedge. At a metalled country lane turn left and follow it as it bears left - do not take the track opposite however inviting it may look! Pass isolated properties and pass through a shady wooded section before bearing right beside an airfield used by light aircraft. The service road running parallel leads to a small light industrial estate.

The road bears away right, signposted Greenstead Green. A short way past the approach drive to Lodge Farm turn off left by a footpath sign into the corner of a rough meadow. Head diagonally over towards the farm where you reach a rough stony track in front of the house. Bear right along it past the moat on your left and farm buildings on the right. Cross over the grass track and head straight over the cultivated field ahead, passing to the right of a round concrete object in the centre. On the far side continue through the next field going slightly left of straight ahead. Pass over a culvert in a gap in the tall hedge and follow the next field boundary left and right to continue beside Tyler's Wood with the church spire at Greenstead Green over on your right. At the end of the field go over the grass to reach a metalled lane at Burton's Green.

Turn left and, after a few yards, right through a gap in the hedge and over a stile along the left side of a field, heading down into the valley with the village of Greenstead Green on the far rise. At the end of the field enter the trees, over a fallen tree trunk, and out again by a stile into a sloping meadow. Head down to leave by a wooden gate into another grazing meadow which you leave immediately via a metal gate on the left. Take the well-worn footpath to a metalled drive opposite a large black barn. Turn right passing a large house and follow its drive as it bends left, ignoring the stile set in metal railings on your right and the path leading down to a lake. Pass the front of Perces and head down to the road on a bend. Carry on over the road bridge spanning Bourne Brook, the course of which we shall now be following for the next two miles. You leave the road by crossing the stile beside the wooden gate on the right just before the bungalow by the village sign. There is a pub about 200 yards further along the road if you require sustenance and are within opening hours.

> The Bourne Brook rises near Wethersfield Airfield and is 10 miles long. It is a sobering thought that, as you follow its course, much of the country-side you will be walking until you meet the A604 was planned to be flooded by damming the brook at Stone Bridge to create a reservoir.

Head through a grazing meadow beside a post and rail fence and then through an open field to reach the trees. Pick up the field edge before entering the wood and passing a sewage plant. The path branches and you take the right fork, leading you out into a cultivated field where you turn right and follow the boundary to the field corner. Turn left and set off along the edge of the field with Bourne Brook on your right initially lined with trees to reach a lane. Turn right and cross the brook by a road bridge.

> There was once a fulling mill here which, in 1823, turned to paper-making before closing and being demolished in 1874.

Go over the stile on the left, now following the right bank through a long meadow. Go over another stile and walk diagonally through a small meadow and then left along the bottom of a sloping meadow. Carry on by a hedge through the next, passing by the end of a long wood at the end. Continue by the hedge through another long meadow and over a plank bridge through a further meadow where a plank bridge leads to a lane. This time you turn left and re-cross the brook before

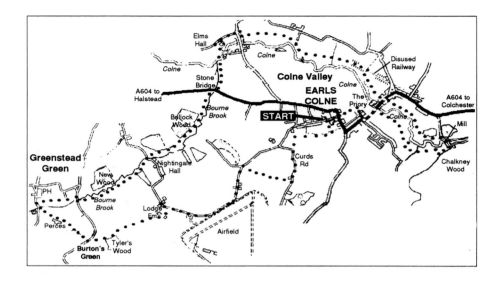

negotiating two stiles beside metal gates to set off through a long meadow now
back following the left bank. You are now bordered on the left by Bullock Wood
and have four meadows to cross linked by stiles. At the end double stiles lead you
into a cultivated field which you cross to another set of stiles on the far side. Bear
left through a metal gate and along a rough meadow to reach the A604 via a stile
set beside another metal gate. Cross with care and turn right along the busy road
to recross the brook again at Stone Bridge.
Escape left over a stepless stile into a meadow. Walk along the left side through
the rough grass beside the wooded brook. A series of crude stiles break your
progress as you continue through meadows with the church tower back at Earls
Colne appearing ahead. Arrive at a cross-hedge and leave by a stile set to the right.
Walk on through rough grass and turn left to cross a major footbridge with
handrails spanning the brook at a point where it joins the river Colne. From here
a winding path through the grass swings right and down a dip. The remains of a
pillar is the only evidence of the brick bridge which once carried the track of the
old railway line. Continue right and over a stile along a meadow to pick up a track
which swings left. Beyond the stile set beside a wooden gate the track is joined by
one leading from a cottage on the left, and you bear right to reach Elms Hall Lane.
Turn right and follow the lane to Jubilee Corner, the junction with Station Road.
Cross the road and the bridged ditch opposite (ignore the footpath sign if it is still
positioned to the right where the ditch is not bridged) and turn right to walk to the
end of the field. Turn left and continue along the field boundary on a well-walked
path. When the field boundary swings right, leave it to continue straight ahead

over the remainder of the field on a well-defined path. **The path divides. Ignoring that forking right to a stile, continue to pick up the right side of the field and then along the edge of a meadow, now given free public access as part of a set-aside policy. A plank bridge leads you along the right side of a field with the river joining you on the right and, beyond it, the golf course. Pass a weir and a track going off left before reaching a wooden gate and post and rail fence. Here you pass to the right of the fence by the river bank and cross a stile on your left to climb the embankment of the disused railway line.**

> The disused railway line was a branch from Haverhill to Chappel on the Sudbury line which, in turn, connected with the main London-Norwich line at Marks Tey.
> It is now preserved as a nature reserve managed by English Nature, along with a mixture of open meadow, scrub and mature trees. The area makes a good site for birds, butterflies and invertebrates, and the cessation of chemical use on, what used to be arable fields, has seen the return of sedges and reeds.

Set off along the shady embankment on a well-worn path. Cross a tributary to the Colne by a wooden footbridge, which has replaced the original railway bridge, and later a track going off left. The next seat, one of several strategically placed along the way, provides a lovely vista across the meadow to the river and golf course beyond, with the church tower in the distance. Soon after you reach a spot with a stile either side of the embankment. Cross the one on the right and walk down beside a wire fence which you follow left, through the meadow, walking parallel with the river to pick up a firm track leading to a stile by the road.
Cross Colneford Hill and turn left. Go right by number 20, beside a brick wall and through a single wooden gate. Continue through rough ground on an overgrown path. Cross a stile and walk along the right side of a meadow beside the Colne. Keep straight ahead at the point where the river swings right and cross another stile and plank bridge leading to another meadow. A bridge with single handrail provides access to a third meadow heading towards Chalkney Mill. Bear left and pass under a pylon and over a stile on to a metalled lane. Turn right, crossing the river and mill pool to reach the mill house.

> This corn mill dates from 1820 and was still operating as recently as 1974. As you pass, note the mill race through an opening in the wall. The mill had a water drop of 2½ metres. The wheel is gone but the axle is still in place.

Go through a wooden gate, past the house and between buildings, to reach Chalkney Wood. Enter the trees on an earthen track and turn immediately right over a footbridge and along a wide path along the edge of the wood. Just beyond a partial clearing, turn right over a plank bridge and stile and down the right side

of a meadow. At the bottom turn left and follow the hedge. Pass under another pylon and bear right to leave the meadow through a solid metal gate. Turn immediately left and walk along the grass between the wire fence and the high hedge for about 40 yards to locate a wide plank bridge. Cross and turn right along the edge of a field and left with the boundary beside a wire fence. At a point where you meet a rough track go over a stepless stile beside a metal gate on the right. Carry on as before passing through a gateway and over a wide culvert. Enter a large grazing meadow and walk along the left side - the river away over on your right. Go over a stile at the end and along a narrow path bordered by a wooden fence and out into the road by the drive of a house.

Turn left along Lower Holt Street bordered on the right by the old wall of the priory. At the service station and the junction with Tey Road (The Coachman Inn Freehouse & Restaurant is on the corner) cross the road with care and take the path beside the metal railings by the entrance to The Priory.

> While very impressive, the Gothic-style red-brick house which has inherited the grand title of The Priory is, in fact, an 18th century building. It does however stand partly on the site of the Benedictine priory founded about 1100-1105 of which virtually nothing remains. Even its greatest treasures, the wonderful 13th and 14th century tombs of the de Veres, Earls of Oxford, were 'removed' in 1935 by neighbouring Suffolk and taken to Bures!

When the railings end by a seat, do not continue ahead over the stile, but instead turn left and take the shady concrete drive to reach the road opposite Park Lane. There is a double bend in the main road here so you will need to cross with extra care before entering Park lane. Before walking the short distance back to your starting point, go through the lychgate and visit the church.

> St Andrews Church is described by Pevsner as 'large but disappointing' although he likes the West tower which looks a little odd with an 18th century brick stair-turret built against the flint 16th century main tower.

THE RIVER COLNE
Walk 6: Wivenhoe to Alresford

Start: *Take the B1027 right off the A133 Colchester to Clacton road and turn right again to Wivenhoe. Park on the free car park just opposite the Greyhound pub as you head down towards the quay.*

O.S.Maps: *Landranger 168; Pathfinder 1077 & 1100.*

Distance: *8½ miles*

Refreshments: *You are best advised to take a drink and snack as, following the Greyhound pub at the start of the walk, there are no refreshment opportunities until The Horse & Groom at beyond two thirds stage.*

Description: *Although this is a long walk it can be terminated when you reach the outskirts of Wivenhoe prior to the northern section. The first section is easy going along the river bank of the Colne and then along Alresford Creek. The second section is much more varied, including minor road, field and woodland, continually interrupted by quarry workings and, after negotiating the northern residential suburbs of Wivenhoe and passing Essex University in Wivenhoe Park, returns to the town by the river.*

LEAVE THE CAR PARK and walk down the street, passing the church to reach the quay.

The villages of Wivenhoe and Rowhedge, on the far side looking right, grew up at the first place where the Colne river valley narrows and offered sheltered anchorages and easy river crossings - being very shallow at this point. Below Wivenhoe the river is comparatively deep, 30-40 feet in parts. Wivenhoe has a proud record in ship and boat building going back to the early 19th century. In 1930 the yard was closed with a forty-year embargo placed on it, but it was re-opened as Wivenhoe Shipyard in World War II and at one time employed 500 shipbuilders building minesweepers and naval craft, with slipways constructed to build craft for the D-Day Normandy Invasion. The shipyard was closed in 1962 although a timber importing wharf was built about 1969 which was later used for small bulk carriers; this enjoyed good business during the boom years of the 1980s.

TURN LEFT AND MAKE YOUR WAY along The Folly, a shingle track, then between empty warehouses to a roadway. Turn right and then left through the car park of the Wivenhoe Sailing Club. There is a modern raised podium with seats where you can come to relax overlooking the new barrage built across the river and watch the activity on the water; but there's no time for that today, so set off along the river bank path away from Wivenhoe past the club-house.

Across the river a quay is engaged in the sole occupation of loading sand and ballast. The area has long provided a rich source for these materials and active quarrying is a common feature on this walk.

There are several seats placed along the way and at one, a rather up-market seat, look for the embankment of a disused railway converging from the left. Named the 'Whelk and Winkle' line, it originally ran along the river's edge to Bright-lingsea. The path swings left and right to join it, heading through a section of woodland. Later go through an opening between two concrete posts to take the path forking right for a short excursion along the river bank itself, snaking by the mudflats to reach a small beach at a point where the river widens. Continue through springy grass dotted with gorse to regain the old railway track, now a path bordered by bushes. When the path forks, bear left between concrete posts; the track continues ahead to end, abruptly, at the mouth of Alresford Creek where the bridge which once spanned it has gone. Continue along the creek to reach an abandoned jetty and the rusting remains of machinery.

Over to your left are the worked-out quarry buildings and evidence of the pulley system which carried buckets of sand and gravel across the field to be unloaded on barges waiting at the jetty. Stackie barges loaded at the ford and at five other places between here and Thorrington Tide Mill until 1914, but from 1932 sailing barges started to load ballast from the jetty. Alresford pit switched to road transport in 1958.

Looking back to the point where the creek enters the main river, you see the ramains of rusting pillars on either side of the creek. These once carried the railway over the creek on a swing bridge which allowed river traffic to enter the creek to load and unload. It was demolished in 1967.

You arrive at a track and go right and left to skirt a house called The Ford. Over on your right is the ford across the river, negotiable at low tide. Continue past the house garden on a raised river bank erected around 1730. It is disappointing to find that, while the path from Wivenhoe has been easy to follow, the council have, up to now at any rate, provided no information along the way by way of history or the flora and fauna inhabiting the river and creeks. Ahead now in the distance on the far side is the impressive tower of Brightlingsea Church (Walk 7). Ignore a footpath which veers off left over a footbridge and carry on until you reach an inlet sending the wall left. Follow it to the end but do not carry on round and back to the creek; instead go down the bank and turn left on a track.

You meet a track coming from Plumpton's Farm on your right. Look straight across the field in front of you to pick out a track coming down on the far side bordered by high hedges. Cross straight over the field to meet it on a bend. This leads to a quarry and as you walk watch out for ballast lorries. Take the path off left im-mediately before the wood and skirt Broomfield Plantation on a well-worn track.

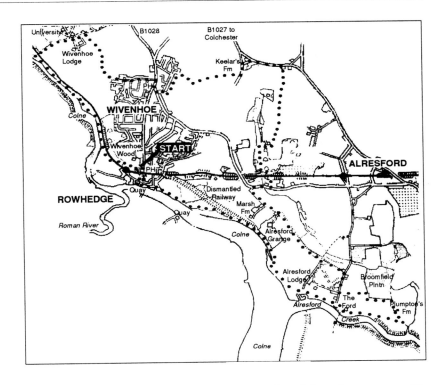

Follow the track right and left, skirting first the wood and then the quarry, with views across the creek and ford over on your left, to reach a country lane.

Turn right and walk past the main quarry buildings. Turn left at Broomlands bungalow along a rough track beside a concrete road passing between lakes created from the exhausted pits. Pass a sign to Alresford Lodge and Creek Lodge, go through a gateway and continue along a track fenced on your right from the stony quarry traffic road created beyond. There are lovely views of the river over on the left and then you pass a large lake on the right, mostly hidden from view. Now your way becomes a delightful shady lane bordered in early summer by bluebells and made the more pleasant if you can close your mind to the quarry road which still runs parallel. Pass the impressive Alresford Grange on your left and then its lodge house. Further on you pass the drive leading to Marsh Farm and arrive at the B1027. Turn right, crossing over at a convenient spot to walk along the wide grass verge. Pass two properties before going left over a stile beyond a metal gate to walk along a narrow path between paddocks. You arrive at the railway track and cross the track via stiles and steps either side of the embankment. Turn left along a footpath heading through the trees. What looks inviting is temporarily interrupted by another active quarry and you are sent left and then right before resuming your woodland walk, initially beside a bubbling brook and even more delightful. The path forks and you take the right. You eventually arrive at a main track on the edge of the trees and turn right. Leaving the wood you pass to the right of a bungalow to reach a cultivated field. Head across the field on a path towards another wood. Turn left just inside the trees. At the end you meet a cross-track by an old oak and turn left. Cross the ditch and turn right. Go over a plank bridge and continue along the right side of the next field. The field boundary swings left and then goes right where you cross another plank bridge to continue along the right side of another field. Continue on the right side of further fields along this well-worn path before crossing an area of rough grass to reach the road.

Turn left and pass the junction on a wide grass verge of the busy B1027. At the right-hand bend turn off left along Keelars Lane passing Keelars Farm on the right. The lane bears left and right and just past the quarry road entrance, look for an opening in the hedge on the right. Take the wide raised path between open fields following the line of telegraph poles. Cross the quarry service road and carry on beyond over the grass beside a lovely large lake - one compensating environmentally-friendly consequence of quarry workings! Meet a track where you turn right and reach a large green. Walk along the right side, either on the green itself or a well-used shady path between hedges and woodland. Turn left at the end of the green to walk along the boundary fences of properties backing on the green. Turn right beyond the last chalet bungalow on a fenced path, with allotments to your left, leading you out to the road opposite the Horse & Groom public house.

Turn right and right again at the roundabout. Cross Colchester Road and turn off left by the Wivenhoe town sign along Heath Road. Cross over Tower Road and Broomfield Crescent and just past the Broome Grove sign on the right take the footpath between numbers 56 and 58.

Cross the road and the path continues past school playing fields. At the end of these it goes right and then left between the walls of houses to come out into a close. Walk a few yards down Jack Hatch Way and look for a wooden gate set back on the right between numbers 11 and 14 where a footpath leads through trees. Ignore the path going left and continue ahead, over a stile, and up an open field, passing under power lines. Go over a stile and continue along the left side of the next field with the tower blocks of Essex University ahead. You reach the university road via a stile; cross over and turn left.

Head down the road and just before it bends right, cross back over to the left-hand side and take the track forking left down through the trees. You reach the railway and cross stiles on either side of the track. Walk on the few yards to reach the river bank. Climb it and turn left. Soon the bank becomes overgrown and at a point where it falls into disuse you take to the metalled lane running between the river and the railway back to Wivenhoe. Later you head through Wivenhoe Wood and

River Colne - Evening calm, Alresford Creek.

the river loops away opposite Rowhedge. A short distance further on turn left to pass under the railway. Do not take the path immediately right running beside the track but go a few yards into the trees and turn right. Now keep straight on to the end of the trees coming out on a small green. Skirt the children's play area and go right to reach the car park and your starting point. There are toilets here.

THE RIVER COLNE
Walk 7: Brightlingsea

Start: *Take the A133 Clacton road from Colchester, then the B1027 right and the B1029 right again to Brightlingsea. Turn right by the war memorial and turn left into Richard Avenue (signposted to the Catholic Church) just past The Brewer's Arms. Park along the road.*

O.S.Maps: *Landranger 168; Pathfinder 1100.*

Distance: *7½ miles*

Refreshments: *Although there is adequate provision for refreshments in town, you are advised to take some refreshment with you as there are no opportunities on the walk itself.*

Description: *Once you have left the built-up area of Brightlingsea the route is a pleasant one of paths, tracks and minor country lanes until you reach the river walll from where you have an easy 3 mile walk back to town along the course of the old 'Whelk & Winkle' railway from Wivenhoe to Brightlingsea.*

IMPORTANT NOTICE: You are advised to avoid this walk until 1998 as the whole length of the river wall is to be closed to walkers from April 1997 until January 1998 for seawall defence work.

COME OUT OF RICHARD AVENUE and turn right. Turn right again opposite the Kings Head into Queen Street. Turn left into Spring Road and second right along Seaview Road. At the T-junction, cross over and turn right for a few yards before turning left beyond the last semi and just before the entrance to the Astralux factory, to take a footpath between a hedge and the factory fence.

Go over a stile into a meadow and head down, bearing left of the copse as the meadow funnels down to a stile at the end. Turn right at the farm along a track towards a pink house. As you approach, the path leads you round to the right and down a shady way through trees. Go over a stile into an old meadow and cross a stream by a substantial footbridge. Go diagonally over the corner of a cultivated field to a plank bridge and stile from where you continue diagonally over a meadow in the same direction, crossing two plank footbridges along the way. In the corner of the meadow turn left and follow the line of trees. The views back over the way you have come are a delightful reminder of how things used to be before modern farming methods turned much of the East Anglian farmlands into prairies. At the end of the meadow a stile beside a gate leads you along a wide grassy track on the right side of a field. Beyond the field a farm track takes you past a wood and, just before reaching the road, at a point where the track turns right, you turn left by a yellow waymark to cross the deep ditch. At the time of my visit there was nothing provided to bridge the ditch or a way through the fence beyond, so I went a few yards further on where the ditch was easier to negotiate and the fence was down in the hedge beyond; perhaps things will have improved on your visit. Turn left in the field for a few yards to the end, then turn half right to head over the next field to the right-hand corner of the wood. Here turn slightly right and walk up the right side of a field with currant bushes growing beyond the fence on your right. At the top do not go over the stile but instead walk along the right side of the meadow beside a wire fence. Turn left at the top for a few yards before going out on to the road. Cross over and turn right, heading for the impressive church which you meet beyond a triangular island on a junction. Your route is left along a quiet metalled 'no through road' signposted to Moverons Farm, but first cross over to pass through the lychgate and visit the church.

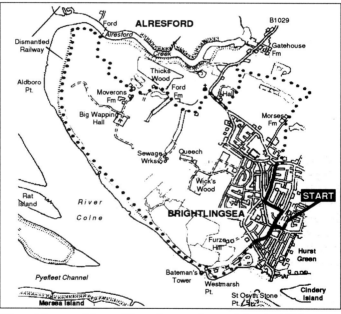

All Saints Church is superbly positioned on an elevated site, its 100 ft tower seen for miles around. Although situated over a mile from town, it is also Brightlingsea's own parish church and beautifully maintained. As Pevsner states, there is ample evidence here of a building much earlier than the one which proudly boasts its Perpendicular prosperity. Roman brickwork in the remains of an Early Norman doorway now embedded in the wall of the South aisle and a blocked lancet window, a doorway in the nave and piers and arches in the South and North arcades, all of 13th century. The church is also rich in 15th and 16th century brasses and monuments.

37

Leave by the gate at the far end of the churchyard and commence an attractive woodland walk albeit along a metalled lane. Watch out for landfill tip lorries. Pass a stretch of water on your left and eventually bear left at the quarry entrance. Continue along a stony track bearing slowly right towards houses with a lake now on your right. When the track bears left towards the farm buildings, you bear right on another track heading down past properties to eventually arrive by the ford at Alresford Creek.

The delights of the river Colne and Alresford Creek have long been appreciated. The house across the creek to your left stands on the site of a Roman villa. Tessellated pavements and painted wall plaster were found when the site was excavated in the 19th century. Up to 1914 stackie barges loaded ballast from Alresford pit at the ford during low tide but from 1932 sailing barges began loading from the more convenient jetty, the rusting remains of which can be seen over to the left on the far shore. Since 1958 transportation has been mainly taken over by road transport.

Turn left and set off along the river wall. At the mouth of the creek where the path bears left look right at the remains of pillars on either bank.

The dismantled railway track of the old Wivenhoe-Brightlingsea railway, affectionatley known as the 'Whelks and Winkles' line follows the river bank back to Brightlingsea. A swing bridge carried the line over Alresford Creek which allowed barges and later craft to use the creek. The bridge was demolished in 1967 leaving the pillars which carried it still remaining.

Set off along the bank for the walk of nearly 3 miles back to Brightlingsea.

The disused railway line forms a nature walkway along the river Colne. Land on either side is listed as a Site of Special Scientific Interest with internationally important intertidal saltmarshes and mudflats on one side and the Brightlingsea Marsh National Nature Reserve on the other.
The saltmarsh and mudflats are of major importance as a food source for wading and other marine birds, and the nature reserve, which is managed by English Nature, is considered to be one of the best coastal grazing marshes remaining in Essex.

You arrive at Brightlingsea by Bateman's Tower.

John Bateman built the tower about 1880 to be used by his family and friends in summer as a bathing hut and in winter as a retreat for wildfowlers caught out on the open marshes.
Brightlingsea is a corporate body of the Cinque Ports and the ancient ceremony connected with the honour is held every year in the tower of the parish church. The main industries here have been yachting, spratting and

oysters. A combination of clean water, correct temperatures and the peculiar fattening qualities which seem to exist here have made the Colne an ideal area for the oyster. Colchester Natives or 'Pyefleets', reckoned by connoisseurs to be the most succulent oyster in the world, are reared here. The oyster industry in Essex estuaries peaked about 1890 when 1,500 men and boys worked in the industry; later, falling numbers of oysters set the Colne Fishing Company in steady decline, and what remained of the Essex oyster population was finally killed off by the hard winter of 1963. The Colchester Oyster Fishery was later set up and began to restore the industry until, in 1982, the oyster was hit by Bonamia disease.

Carry on along the promenade past the children's paddling pool and beach huts and turn left after the swimming pool and immediately before the large boating lake to reach the road. Turn right and keep straight on, passing the Leisure Village, to enter Station Road. Pass the Co-op to arrive back in the centre by the War Memorial (toilets are situated along the way). Right will take you back to Richard Avenue, your starting point.

THE RIVER COLNE & COAST
Walk 8: St Osyth

Start: *Take the A133 road to Clacton from Colchester and B1027 turning right to St Osyth. Turn right at the end of the old priory wall along The Bury and park in the Priory car park on the right.*

O.S.Maps: *Landranger 169; Pathfinder 1101.*

Distance: *3½ or 9½ miles*

Refreshments: *There are pubs and restaurants in St Osyth but no refreshment opportunities on the walk itself except at Seawick during the summer season.*

Description: *The short walk involves a track to St Osyth Boating Lake followed by a fine walk along the bank of the lake and St Osyth Creek. You return via a nature reserve and a modest road walk. To include the length of St Osyth beach, marsh and mudflats, the full walk involves a 2 mile road walk to Seawick and a section of tough pathless and signless field walking. Added to the fact that there are no information boards along the way and no way back to the path at Lee-over-Sands if you wished to walk along the beach itself, the facilities for the walker in this area leave much to be desired.*

TAKE THE STONY TRACK which leads off opposite the Priory car park marked by a footpath sign. After a few paces a footpath forks right.
FOR THE SHORT 3½ MILE WALK ignore the path forking left and carry straight on along the stony track. Later it bears left and right to skirt Warren Farm and continues down to the causeway across the boating lake. Do not cross it but instead turn right to follow the right bank. (Details of the route from this point continue from * on the long walk description).
FOR THE FULL WALK take the path forking left at the start and continue past the churchyard. Carry on along the left side of a cultivated field. When the path divides go left, still following the left side of the field. Go left at the end past buildings to reach the road opposite Brook Vale. Turn right and set off along Spring Road for a walk of nearly 2 miles to the holiday village of Seawick. Initially you are on a footpath, but as the road crosses a pretty stream and heads up Beach Road, the footpath ends and you must continue along the road edge.
With much relief you eventually arrive at Seawick an extraordinary place comprised entirely of static holiday homes and the facilities provided to service them. Climb the promenade and turn right to set off along the seawall. (If you wish to visit the beach do so here as there is no way back across the marsh and mudflats further on). The wall gradually veers away from the beach and the area of mudflats increases. On your right is the expanse of St Osyth Marsh.
You reach the isolated collection of timber chalets and cross the little service road which leads past the sewage works to Lee Wick Farm. Continue past the scattered

buildings, most of which stand empty and abandoned - out of season at any rate. The river bank bears right as you enter the Colne Estuary.

> Brightlingsea Estuary comprises the estuary of the river Colne. Between the river bank and the estuary are about 400 acres of Colne Point mudflats which form an Essex Naturalist's Trust reserve for brent geese, sanderlings, curlew, redshanks and little tern.
> Beyond is Ray Creek where, from 1930 to 1957, barges loaded shingle brought from the point on a narrow gauge railway to the creek's Barge Pier.

When you have passed the sewage works go down the bank and cross the field ahead to reach the access road. Head over the narrow field beyond and cross into the next over a culvert. Now head to the right of the small ruined barn and locate another culvert. Beyond this the official right of way goes straight ahead through the next field but as there is nothing to help you find the route after this I suggest that you bear right to pick up the bank of a water course. Now stay with this as it winds its way along the edge of the field to the point where it suddenly ends.

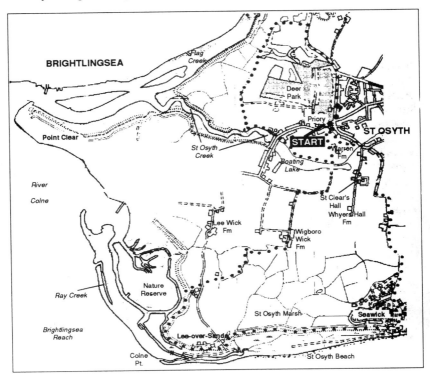

Crossing your way is another water course. Turn right and follow the line of this along the left side of another field with the grain silos of Wigboro Wick Farm ahead and to your left. Later you have a line of shrubs and bushes on your left before picking up the farm track which goes left, heading between the farm buildings. The track becomes a metalled lane bordered by hedges. When the lane turns left, go right along a track between open fields. After 400 yards take the track left, still between open fields, to reach a causeway taking the track between the appropriately named Reed Pond on the right and the lovely St Osyth Boating Lake on the left. Immediately beyond this turn left to join the short walk * along a well-walked path beside the lake with a cultivated field on the right. You pass a landing stage used by water skiers and cross the road.

> While quaint, the mixture of modern boats and rotting hulks which occupy the old quay is evidence that the river trade at Osyth, locally pronounced 'Toosey' has had its highs and lows. On the first bend of St Osyth Creek a dock had been constructed in 1932 to transport sand from a nearby pit, but this was soon abandoned. The Tide Mill of 1730 fell down in 1962. The mill barge dock had a low 'half tide' quay to enable carts to back up to barges at deck level. In the 30s slump 22 sailing barges were laid up at the head of the creek. In 1946 it was developed as a boatyard, the quay extended and raised and the old mill pool became a lake for water sports.

Walk through the quay and on along a path atop the river bank. After about 500 yards look for a path going right up the right side of a cultivated field. You join a stony track and head down to a gate leading you beside Howlands Marsh, a Nature Reserve created by the Essex Wildlife Trust. Carry on past Nun's Wood and at the end, confronted by the entrance to a quarry and landfill site, turn right to follow the edge of the wood. While still a very pleasant walk on a well-used path, it is soon tainted by the intrusion of the landfill activity beyond the fence on your left. With lovely parkland over on the right as you climb away from the trees this must at one time have been a delightful footpath. Eventually you come out on the B1027, cross over and turn right. This is a busy road but the wide grass verge makes it safe and easy going. At Lamb Farm House, cross over and take the footpath right into St Osyth. You pick up and follow the priory precinct wall and, at the crossroads, turn right back to your starting point and a possible visit to the Priory.

> St Osyth was the daughter of the first Christian king of the East Angles. She was martyred in 653 near the place of the present Priory, where she had founded a nunnery, of which nothing now remains. The priory (later abbey) was established for Augustinian canons by Richard de Belmeis, Bishop of London, shortly before 1127. A few fragments remain from this period and a few more from the 13th century. The most impressive remains are the magnificent late 15th century gatehouse.

The Rivers Pant & Blackwater

The sun is falling in fragments
clouds in marquetry.
Leave silhouettes upon
the silently distending disc.
Mist blends horizon
and foreground like a blind
drawing down on the river.
Between the banks
a sheer pink plane,
flat, lifeless
but for the slowly
cooling colour
deepening into dusk.

('Blackwater Sunset' - Barry Norrington)

THE PANT, which rises at Frogs Green on the edge of Wimbush Parish, was originally the name of the river from source to sea at Sales Point, Bradwell. It is only since about 1848 when White's map was produced that a section downstream from King's Bridge at Bocking has been called The Blackwater. The Pant was mentioned in Bede's *'Historia Ecclesiastica'* as early as the 8th century and in the famous poem *'The Battle of Maldon'* composed after the battle of 991. Norden's map of 1594 set a precedent, however, by calling the whole length of the river 'Blackwater', with the 'Pante' being described as only a 'smalle river', and this is how it has been viewed since. On the ground, the contrast between the two during the walks is very evident; the Pant meandering its way as little more than a stream through peaceful water meadow, while the Blackwater, broad and expansive, provides the commercial waterway to the sea.

The whole river is 36 miles long and was canalised in its lower section in 1793 to form the Chelmer & Blackwater Navigation (see page 78).

The River Pant at Great Bardfield (Walk 9).

THE RIVER PANT
Walk 9: Finchingfield, Wethersfield & Gt.Bardfield

Start: *Finchingfield is best reached by the B1053 from Saffron Walden (off the M11) or the B1057 off the A604 Colchester to Haverhill road. In the village, park along the lane (one-way) which runs along the back of, and overlooks the Green.*

O.S.Maps: *Landranger 167; Pathfinder 1051.*

Distance: *8½ miles*

Refreshments: *There are pubs and restaurants in Finchingfield itself and you will pass Dicken's Restaurant in Wethersfield and at least one tea room and two pubs in Great Bardfield along the way.*

Description: *For the most part the walk follows the course of the meandering River Pant through grazing meadows, along field paths, farm tracks and quiet country lanes. With care the route, although quite intricate, is easy to follow and rarely out of sight of the river. It's well worth spending a little time to relax in Finchingfield, one of Essex's loveliest villages, when your walk is over.*

COMMENCE THE WALK BY setting off along the little one-way lane in which you are parked and then along the street passing the Post Office. A little way past turn down a metalled path. Do not cross the footbridge over Finchingfield Brook but turn right just before it, along a narrow path running beside the brook and with the rear of properties on your right. Continue through a section of woodland and then by paddocks. Follow the left side of a cultivated field then over a plank bridge and stile into a meadow. Beyond this a stile leads you into a further long meadow. Cross a stile and track bearing right and left to continue on along the left side of a field signposted 'to Gt.Bardfield Watermill'.

When the field boundary commences to bear right, leave it by going left over a plank and stile (by another sign pointing back to Finchingfield) to cross a narrow grazing meadow. Go over another stile and major footbridge across the Brook. Cross another small grazing meadow then break from the official route, which is impossible to follow through the fenced paddocks, by going left to locate a wooden farm gate leading you on to a track. Turn right and at the entrance gates displaying the name 'Champions' and 'Beware of the dog', turn left along a grassy track between wooden post fencing. At the top turn right along a grass track with a fence enclosing a large grazing meadow on your right; there are fine views from here. At the end of the field on your right meet a metalled country lane on a bend and turn right along it towards Robjohns Farm.

As you approach turn left along a stony track towards the entrance gates to a house. Immediately in front of them climb the bank on your left and continue along the right side of a cultivated field for a short distance to an opening on the right. Turn right and walk along the right side of another field. You pass the shingle drive and grounds of the house and beyond it the large man-made lake. When the internal corner goes right, turn left and set off across the open field, walking slightly right of parallel with the hedgerow away on your left. It will not matter if you are a little out as, on the far side, you just drop down the bank on to a country lane and turn right to walk to Sculpin's Bridge, carrying the lane over the river Pant.

Turn left and continue along the left bank as it follows a meandering course through the fields. Stay with it until, after you go right on a very raised bank and then left, the river bends right again towards the field corner. Do not follow it right but carry straight on cutting off the end of the field and reaching a wide green track beyond bordered by wire fences with the raised bank enclosure and buildings of Anglian Water on your left. Carry on, the track now hedged, to reach the road by the plant entrance gates.

Turn right for a few yards then left along the right side of a field. Carry straight on through an open field to a footbridge on the far side. The way continues on a grass track between open fields, then along the right side to reach a drive to a leaded-windowed house. Turn right on to a fenced path which goes left by a grazing meadow, passing behind the detached garage block of another house with leaded windows. Go over a stile and up the gravel entrance drive, between paddocks to reach the road.

Turn right along Saffron Gardens to enter Wethersfield. Pass the Post Office Stores and several interesting properties including The Gables. Reach a small green and road junction and turn right along Old Mill Chase, a 'No Through Road', by Dicken's Restaurant. Beyond the restaurant car park a narrow path weaves its way round the school playground and out into a small close of modern houses.

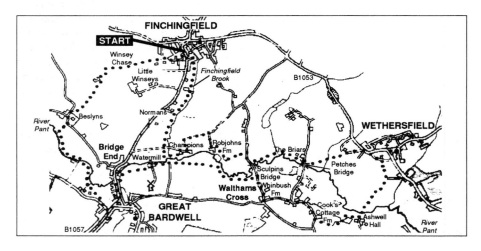

Carry on to the junction and turn left for a few yards before crossing the road and taking a well-worn footpath heading away along the left side of a field. Pick up a track and go right and left. After a short distance it goes right again. The official line is to leave it and head straight across the field ahead but if it is under crop or deep ploughed, making it difficult, follow the track right and left to reach the river again. Turn right and follow the right bank to the large, unusual concrete footbridge, which you cross. Do not keep ahead on to Ashwell Hall but instead turn immediately right over a stepless stile to follow the left bank for a few yards. As it bears right leave the river and head across the rough grass to a metal gate in the left-hand corner. Follow the left side of the field as it bends left, then cross the dip on your left and turn right to continue along the right side of a field by a section of woodland. Keep to the woodland to reach a quiet country lane via the grounds of Cook's Farm Cottage and turn right.

Follow this attractive wooded lane, bearing left at the junction signposted to Gt.Bardfield and passing a bungalow called The Hollies. At the junction turn right heading down hill and passing Whinbush Farm. Just beyond the end of the woodland on your right is an opening into a field in which stands a pill-box. Opposite, on your left, is a footpath by a metal gate in the hedge. Go through it and cross a stile and head down over the parkland. Go through the gateway and up the long meadow beyond to a stile in the far right-hand corner. Go over thia and another to return to the river bank. Set off through old meadows parallel with the Pant. Go over a stile and plank bridge and continue along the right side of a cultivated field. Just before the river bends left, you turn left along a path through the open field, at first parallel with the river, and beyond it a stretch of water. The river bears right and then left to stay parallel with your path but well over to the right. You can see Robjohn's Farm and then Champions, encountered on your outward journey, and the windmill at Great Bardfield appears to the left of straight ahead. Cross a stile by a metal gate and continue through a rough grass meadow. Carry on through the next meadow with the river over on your right. Head diagonally right to reach a stile by a transformer on a telegraph pole. Pass to the right of a sewage plant and head along the right side of a field beside the river - the windmill now over on your left. At the end go through the hedge and turn right on the drive in front of the old watermill for a detour of a few yards to the bridge.

> This is the point where the Pant takes on more substantial dimensions and up until about fifty years ago drove Great Bardfield Mill. Thomas S Smith bought the mill in 1894, along with the windmill, but the two mills had been linked since 1754 when Jonas Osborne bought the windmill having leased the watermill since 1742. The great water-wheel still remains.

Back along the track turn right beyond the mill house and set off through the meadow heading for a massive old oak tree in the far left-hand corner. Carry on along the left side of the next meadow which funnels down to a stile and a well-worn path beside a cultivated field. As you reach the first property beyond the river on the right, cross the plank bridge and walk between houses to reach the road. Turn left and walk into Great Bardfield.

At the junction turn right to Thaxted and Dunmow and pass The Vine, a possible refreshment stop. Walk up the street passing the cross and turn right along the road to Little Bardfield almost opposite another temptation, The Bell. Pass Durham Close and the thatched Bell Cottage which does B&B. On the bend take the footpath sign right and take the left fork over a stile and down a meadow. Cross a stile by the left-hand hedge and continue down the remainder of the meadow. Go over a stile in the left-hand corner and cross a large plank footbridge into another meadow. Head diagonally across and go over a stile by a wooden gate and diagonally over the next meadow. Negotiate another stile which leads you along a well-used path along the right side of a field to meet the river Pant again.

As you approach farm buildings at Mill House cross the river by a concrete footbridge to carry on, now along the right bank past grazing cattle.

Later go over a stile by a weir at Copford Hall pumping station. Press on along a path of rough grass and just past a footbridge on your left, go over a stile ahead and turn right to walk up the right side of a meadow away from the river and heading towards Beslyns in its wooded grounds. Cross a stile leading into a country lane and turn left and right to skirt the grounds. The lane goes off left to Little Bardfield at Beslyn's Stable and you carry straight on, signposted Pitley Farm. Pass Beslyn's Cottage and take the footpath right along a track through meadowland. The faint grassy track divides and you bear left by an internal corner. The track then continues along the left side of a cultivated field. At the end of the field, leave the track and go over a footbridge just to the right, set in the hedge. Carry on along the left side of a field going through a hedge at the end and over another footbridge. Turn left to the end of the field and pick up the track again, going right between high hedges. Go over a cross-track and keep with your grassy track which follows the field boundary left and right.

This wide grassy track is called Winsey Chase and it will lead you in various forms straight back to Finchingfield. You arrive in the village and turn left to walk the few paces back to your starting point.

A walk down and across the Green, perhaps to get refreshments and look around, re-introduces you to the Pant, here at its widest. The river plays its own part in making this probably the most photographed village in Essex. The church has a Norman West tower and much of interest while, beside it, the timber-framed Guildhall has stood here since c1500.

THE RIVER PANT
Walk 10: Radwinter, Wimbush & Wimbush Green

Start:	*Take the B1053 from Saffron Walden or the B1057 and B1054 from Haverhill and park by the church in Radwinter.*
O.S.Maps:	*Landranger 154; Pathfinder 1050 & 1051.*
Distance:	*6 miles*
Refreshments:	*Pub in Radwinter, but the only one on the walk is off the route at Howlett End.*
Description:	*The early part of the walk follows the bank of the youthful river Pant as far as Clay Wood. The walk then goes by quiet country lanes to Wimbush Green, after which field paths lead you back to meet the Pant at Adcock's Lane. The next section following the Pant along the wide 'ride' of an ancient meadow is the highlight of the walk. From Mill Road near Wimbush Hall the meandering river bank is followed beside cultivated fields to Radwinter, arriving back via the churchyard and the old vicarage of c1500.*

SET OFF ALONG THE B1054, past the church and over the crossroads with the B1053. At the river bridge turn right off the road and follow the right bank of the river Pant. The path divides and you go over the footbridge to head diagonally left to reach a stepless stile. Carry on through the next meadow past a metal gate and over a concrete culvert. Carry on by the river along the right side of a meadow and then on a wide green track by a cultivated field. At a point where the field ends at a track which is carried over the river by a concrete cart bridge, turn left on the track but at the top of the field instead of following it left, go over the metal gate on your right and set off along a long narrow pasture, the river over on your right. A stepless stile at the end leads you through an area of rough grass to pick up the river bank again.

Cross the river by a substantial footbridge and head away between open fields, picking up a track along the right side of Clay Wood, climbing steadily. Keep the hedge on your left to reach a track and then turn right on a metalled lane by the entrance to Little Brockholds Farm.

Pass the drive leading to Great Brockholds Farm before meeting a country road on a bend. Carry straight on to Wimbush Green, turning left and then following the bend right by two willow trees and a lovely thatched house called Nottages into Lower Green. You pass several fine detached properties and after Mill House the road is unmade. Following the last white house on the left it becomes a grassy track passing through an area of green and scattered scrub to reach another section of metalled country road. Follow the road round to the right (ignore the concrete footpath sign pointing left) passing Lower House Farm and go over a green metal gate on the left by a wooden footpath sign into a meadow.

Head straight over the meadow and through a gap in the far hedge crossing a deep ditch. There was no plank on my visit but at least it was dry! Walk straight over the cultivated field ahead to the end of the hedge line, left of a double telegraph pole. Carry on straight over the next field again to the end of the tree line and continue to reach a cross track. Right is towards the water tower, but you turn left for a few yards then right to follow the stream passing a culvert and picking up a grass track. The track swings right and you leave it to continue straight ahead on a grassy path which then goes over a culvert switching to the left bank. At the end of the field turn right to recross the stream and pick up the hedge bordering the field on the right for about 30 yards before following it left and then bearing right. At the end, locate a little metalled path and turn right to reach the road, hedge on right. Cross Mill Road and set off on a wide grassy track down the left side of the field to the right to commence the most delightful section of the whole walk.

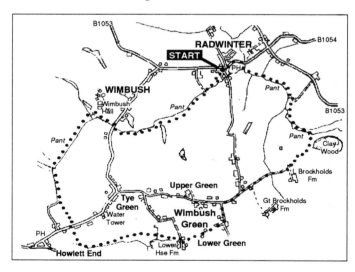

At the end of the field walk through an area of rough grass and enter the edge of a small copse. Here you cross a footbridge beside a little ford straddling a bubbling brook - what a lovely tranquil spot! Beyond the trees you meet a wide grassy ride and turn right to follow it. At the end of the field on your left, Adcock's Lane swings left and you leave it for something even better. A grassy path forks right through the trees into a narrow meadow which opens out into a delightful grassy ride bordered by ancient trees and hedges and accompanied by the perky little River Pant down on your right.

All good things come to an end and eventually you leave via a culvert as the ride opens out into a lovely meadow. The farm buildings of Wimbush Hall, and beyond the hall itself, the little towerless church, appear ahead as you gradually bear right with the river.

> Rookery Pond, a lake enclosed by tall trees, is over to the left with the hall, now a farmhouse on the site of the old hall which was burnt down in 1952, straight ahead. Beyond it you can just make out the Norman church, without its brick tower since 1883.

Cross a culvert over the river and go through a wooden gate on the left and along a short stretch of green lane, the river running below the raised bank on your left, to reach Mill Road again.

The river passes under the road bridge and you cross the road and go over the stile to the right and go left and right round the field edge to return to the river bank. You set off following the river and it winds its way below steep banks by fields for some way. Eventually the boundary makes a sharp turn left and then right into the corner of the field where you arrive at a footbridge crossing the river and a yellow waymark directing a footpath over it. Do not cross, but instead follow the field boundary right and then left to reach another cross path at another internal field corner. This time turn left through a gap in the hedge and cross diagonally right over the meadow towards a wide concrete culvert. Cross the river here and turn right along a grassy track along the left side of a cultivated field, beside the Pant on your right.

The hedge on the right ends and the river flows free through open countryside with the spire of Radwinter Church appearing ahead. Pass a quaint brick bridge and pick up a post and rail fence on your left. Bear left with the fence on a path which passes through an area of rough grass then heads down and across a meadow, passing the churchyard over on your left. Go through a wooden gate and over a footbridge to pick up the drive leading to the church. Turn left to enter the churchyard with the old vicarage claiming to be of c1500 date on your left.

> The first thing that strikes you about the Church of St Mary the Virgin is the remarkable early 14th century porch which was thankfully left by Eden Nesfield when he virtually rebuilt the church in 1869, although it was he who added the pretty domestic upper storey. There is fine flushwork to the main body of the church and to the West tower added in 1887. There are other parts dating back to the 14th century and a 15th century painting. A famous encumbant here was William Harrison who published his 'Description of England' in 1577. Born in 1534, he was rector for 34 years from 1559.

The River Blackwater at Abbey Mill, Coggeshall (Walk 11).

THE RIVER BLACKWATER
Walk 11: Coggeshall Hamlet to Bradwell

Start: *Coggeshall is situated on the A120 between Colchester and Braintree. Take the B1024 road into town and south towards Kelvedon. After just over half a mile, park on the shingle parking area on the small green on the left at Coggeshall Hamlet.*

O.S.Maps: *Landranger 168; Pathfinder 1076.*

Distance: *6 or 9 miles.*

Refreshments: *There is a pub at Bradwell, and pubs and cafes in Coggeshall just off the walk.*

Description: *After a short walk along field paths you have a virtually traffic-free 2 mile jaunt along a narrow metalled country lane. From here the tracks and field paths to Bradwell to meet he river Blackwater can be omitted to shorten the walk by a third. You then follow the course of the river except for two short flirtations with the A120 and a stretch of track on the Essex Way. The last section is, in many ways, the most interesting. You first pass the remains of Coggeshall Abbey and then walk the most delightful stretch of the river bank between Abbey Mill and Pointwell Mill back to Cogggeshall Hamlet.*

WALK BACK ALONG THE ROAD and after the last house on the left, take the concrete service road. Pass to the left of the Eastern Electricity sub-station enclosure and take the path along the left side of a field which then switches to the right side of the field on your left via a plank footbridge. The way then continues as a farm track between open fields to reach Cuthedge Lane.

Turn right and follow this quiet little lane for nearly 2 miles as it meanders through open deserted countryside. Later it bears right heading down into the Blackwater valley. At a point where it bends sharp left a grass track continues on down towards the river. If you wish to shorten your walk to 6 miles and missing out Bradwell you will leave the lane here and take the track, picking up the directions from point *.

For the full walk follow the lane left and down passing under the power lines just to the right of a point where the pylons make a 90° turn to the right. At the bottom of the hill turn left along the Essex Way, the concrete approach road to a quarry works. Bear right of the large grass-covered spoil hill across the grass and through a plantation of young trees to reach a minor road.

Cross and take the footpath sign just to the left, heading through a cultivated field and passing by the right end of Jubilee Plantation. Carry on ahead to reach a grass track. The Essex Way goes left but you turn right along the track passing under power lines again to reach another minor road at Perry Green.

Turn left , passing the turning to Cressing and Silver Street with Hill House and Perry Green Farm on your left. The road bends left and right and you cross the grass to cut off the corner. Just after the next left-hand bend take the footpath right along the left side of a field. At the bottom a stile beside a wooden gate leads you to a meadow. Walk along the left side and leave by another stile beside a wooden gate in the corner. Turn right along the field, cutting off the corner and making for a gap between two lines of fences bordering the gardens of properties lining the street at Bradwell, a village shown on maps until quite recent times as Blackwater. Cross the road and go a few paces right to walk down the left side of the field opposite. Follow the field boundary as it bends left and then cross a plank bridge leading to a playing field. Walk down the right side and exit at the bottom through an opening. Carry on down to the footbridge over the River Blackwater. Turn left and walk beside the fence and then go right to cross another footbridge by an attractive mill pool and weir.

Continue up the path to reach the A120 near Blackwater Bridge. Turn right and walk along the busy road to a point where a footpath sign sends you right, along the far edge of the grassed area at the end of the service station. After a few yards

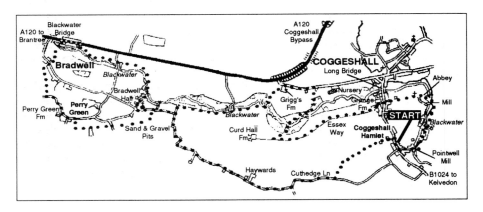

look for a place to scramble down the bank to the field on the left and continue down the right side to the end. Turn left and walk along the bottom edge of this field and the two following fields, crossing the access road to the quarry. An area of rough grass, trees and scrub separates you from the river on the right. Beyond the fields you continue along a wide grass strip now beside the river to reach a concrete bridge. Cross the river here and head up a track between the buildings of Bradwell Hall to reach the road and church.

Attractively crude, the little Church of Holy Trinity, set apart from the village along with the hall, certainly looks old, and is. Mainly Norman with

Roman brick trim, its most interesting feature is the wall paintings which, although not well-preserved and proving difficult to expose without causing further damage, are of fine quality and date from about 1320. There is a 16th century monument to Anthony Maxey and his family.

Set off along Cuthedge Lane again towards Coggeshall, and from the valley retrace your steps past the entrance to the quarry works, up the hill and under the power lines to reach the bend where we left the short walk *.
Turn off down the grassy track and follow it bearing right, a little way short of the river, now progressing through the long grass and light woodland on a less well-defined path. You pass a delightful stretch of water and continue on a narrow path through the grass and on along the left side of a field. At the end of the field pass to the left of the security fence enclosing the gravel works and on by a post and rail fence, walking parallel with the unmade access road. Ignore a yellow waymark arrow pointing right for the Essex Way, and carry on now beside a wire fence. Ignore the stiles and arrows placed one each side of the road and keep on until you reach green painted metal kissing gates situated either side just prior to the river bridge. Cross here and continue in the same direction as before, crossing the river on a footbridge. Continue along the grass to the point where a group of young trees have been planted. Look for a stile partially hidden in the hedge on the right and from here head diagonally up the cultivated field, making for a stile in the far corner just to the left of Grigg's Farm. You come out on the old Coggeshall Road just east of the A120 bypass and turn right.
At the end of a group of houses on the left, turn right into the car park of Coggeshall Youth Football Club ground and walk down the left side joining a track which leads down to the Blackwater. Bear right and follow the often overgrown river bank to a point where a footbridge takes you over and away on a clear, if meandering, path through a meadow making for the far right hand corner. A small footbridge here takes you into a field and you follow the left side up to meet a firm, wide track. Turn left along the Essex Way which takes you to the road past the buildings of Grange Farm.

The fully restored and impressive 130 feet long Tithe Barn over on your left as you approach the road, with its king-post roof, dates from c1500 and is a remarkable survival.

There are other equally interesting historic remains just ahead. Cross the road and take Abbey Lane opposite. Standing alone, beyond the houses, you pass a chapel before reaching Abbey Farm and other remains of the Abbey.

The Chapel of St Nicholas was a gatehouse chapel, built in 1225, for the Cistercian Abbey founded by King Stephen about 1140. No trace of the church has been found above ground, but as at Beeleigh, (see Walk 18), a 16th century house has been built into the major part of what remains; while no doubt practical, it is a little disconserting to see the rest acting as farm storage buildings.

Bearing left between the buildings, the track crosses the river on a bridge above Abbey Mill and then over 'The Back Ditch'.

> The river was diverted from 'The Back Ditch', its original course, by the monks from the abbey to create a wider stretch of water to operate a mill; the bridge is from this period (13th century).
> The present Abbey Mill was rebuilt on the site of an earlier mill in the 17th century.

Bear right over the rough grass following the line of the virtually stagnant 'Black Ditch' and, at a point where it becomes neatly lawned, the main river joins you from the mill.

Cross a footbridge by a weir and a little further on you arrive at another mill back at Coggeshall Hamlet, passing through a gate and skirting the mill house.

> After becoming redundant in 1902, Pointwell Mill was sold off and used as a milk store until 1933. In 1960, when virtually derelict, it was converted to a home.

Take the lane back up to the road and turn right. The road is rather blind at this point and there is no footpath initially, so take care. After a few yards you can regain the footpath as you arrive at the little green, your starting point.

THE RIVER BLACKWATER
Walk 12: Tollesbury

Start: *Take the B1023 Kelvedon slip road off the A12 road between Colchester and Chelmsford and park in the market place.*

O.S.Maps: *Landranger 168; Pathfinder 1099 & 1123.*

Distance: *8 miles.*

Refreshments: *Pubs in Tollesbury but no refreshment opportunities on the walk itself.*

Description: *A very easy walk for all seasons with easy parking in the centre of Tollesbury. Follow a track for over a mile leading you straight to the river. A raised river wall then takes an irregular course tracing the bank of the Blackwater towards the estuary and then along the South Channel of Tollesbury Fleet and around Woodrolfe and Old Hall Creeks.*

WALK ALONG THE MARKET PLACE passing the church and leading on to a track which heads away for over a mile to reach the river wall. Turn left and set off to follow the Blackwater towards the estuary passing Mill Point, a small island. The wall then sweeps left to take you round Mill Creek with Mell Farm set back. As you round the creek and head back to the river proper you will notice a low bank running parallel over on your left and, as you meet the river again and turn left , you pass the point where it ends and will recognise it as a disused railway track.

Tollesbury was the terminus of the light railway which ran from Kelvedon and affectionately known as the Crab & Winkle Line. Opened in 1904, it was extended to the bank of the Blackwater in 1907 when a wooden pier was built here. Although oysters were the chief industry along the river, the commercial interest in this case was jam. Arthur Wilkin established his fruit farm at nearby Tiptree and built a jam-making factory in 1885. It stayed open until 1921, with the passenger service continuing to Tollesbury until 1951, and goods until 1962.

Mells is the early spelling of mill and with Mill Creek and Mill Point there is little doubt that once a tide mill operated an earlier industry here.

On your left now are the peaceful and atmospheric marshes of Tollesbury Wick now managed by the Essex Wildlife Trust. The square bulk of Bradwell nuclear power station looms ever larger over on the far bank as you head for Shinglehead Point. Ahead on the estuary before you turn inland is Mersea Island. Follow the South Channel of Tollesbury Fleet with the lightship and the masts of yachts at Tollesbury Marina appearing ahead to the left as you pass Great Cob Island. The wall eventually turns left into Woodrolfe Creek and you pass through the marina.

At the end turn right and walk along the footpath by the harbour then past modern white wood-cladded link houses before going down a set of concrete steps to the road. Cross over and climb the steps beyond to walk between boatyards and back along the river wall. At Tollesbury Fleet the wall has been diverted.

> This sea defence set-back trial is being operated by English Nature. It involves building a new sea wall at a more inland location, then breaching the old wall to allow salt marsh to return to the intervening land. The new saltmarsh will act as a natural defence and help replace saltmarshes lost to erosion and historical reclamations in the Tollesbury Fleet.

At a point where the wall turns right, a shingle drive comes up to meet you and you leave the bank to turn left and follow it straight back to the town, crossing the B1023 and entering the market place, your starting point.

> St Mary's Church is of ancient origin with an 11th century nave and West tower. A Norman window has a representation in modern glass of St Cedd, the Saxon bishop who built the first churches in Essex. The font was obtained in 1718 by churchwarden Robert Joyce from a John Norman who came into church cursing and talking during service. To prevent his being prosecuted he paid £5, and out of this sum the font was bought, the churchwarden having the following inscription added: 'Good people all, I pray take care That in the church you do not swear. As this man did'.
>
> Still remaining in the market square, situated in the NW corner of the churchyard, is the Lockup, a temporary place of detainment for local criminals.

THE RIVER BLACKWATER
Walk 13: Mundon to Maylandsea

Start: *Take the road to Maldon leaving the bypass on the B1018 towards Burnham. In the village of Mundon park in the area of the White Horse pub - in a layby or possibly in the car park of the pub itself if you intend to partake of their services.*

O.S.Maps: *Landranger 168; Pathfinder 1123.*

Distance: *9½ miles.*

Refreshments: *The only opportunity is at the White Horse at the beginning and end of your walk so being a longish walk it is better to carry some refreshments with you.*

Description: *A very contrasting walk in respect of the going and difficulty in route finding. You lead off on a track but encounter sections of cross-field walking before reaching the sanctuary of the river wall. You follow the meandering wall for over five miles before again facing open fields with limited direction markers and a disputed course across the lands of Mundon Hall - although I hasten to add that the owners are not anti-walkers and are trying to find the best and most convenient route.*

WALK ALONG THE B1018 away from the pub and turn left along West Chase. Carry on beyond the metalled close along a rough straight track which leads to a narrow metalled country lane on a bend (you will return this way).

Carry straight on and when the lane bends right towards Mundon Hall, leave it to cross a stile and walk over a meadow to the end of the hedge line. Turn left and continue along the right side of a cultivated field. Go over a footbridge and cross an area of rough grass bearing right and left to continue along the left side of a field to reach a country road to the left of White House Farm. Cross over and go a few yards left to pick up a grassy track along the right side of a field. At the end cross a concrete culvert over Mundon Wash.

> An enterprising farmer, John Marriage, from nearby White House Farm, built his own canel in 1820, based on the course of the Mundon Wash, to take out his produce and bring in coal and manure via the Blackwater. Though disused and derelict by the end of the century Anglian Water re-established it in the 1970s as part of a drainage scheme.

Head straight across the field ahead to another culvert, this one grass, over a ditch. Cross a large cultivated field to a plank bridge leading into another field. Turn left and walk a short distance to pick up a waymark sign which sends you once again straight over the cultivated field on your right. On the far side cross the culvert via a gap in the hedge and cross a stony farm track leading to Bramble Hall Farm to take the wide grassy track opposite, following the right side of a field. There are good views across to Maldon ahead.

Cross another concrete culvert and turn left to walk over the field to a footbridge with metal handrails. Now follow the left side towards a bungalow situated to the left of the buildings of South House Farm. Pick up a grass track along the left side of the next field running parallel with the B1018, away over on your left, lined with properties all with dormer windows. At the end of the field the grassy track bears right with the boundary and you continue ahead over a culvert and through a field, aiming just to the left of the bungalow. In the corner of the field by a row of fir trees, a stile leads you into and through a mini meadow out on to a metalled lane. Turn right and pass between farm buildings and the impressive South House. Beyond the farm the lane eventually ends not only at the Blackwater river bank at Southey Creek but also a place of great historic importance.

> The following entry in the *Anglo-Saxon Chronicle* gives a bare outline of the events surrounding 'The Battle of Maldon' fought between the Saxons and Vikings: 'In this year Olaf came with 93 ships to Folkstone, and ravaged round about it, and then from there went to Sandwich, and so from there to Ipswich, and overran it all, and so to Maldon. And Earldorman Brihtnoth came against him; and they killed the earldorman there and had control of the field.' We would know little of this epic battle, fought on August 10th 991 A.D. were it not the subject of two surviving contemporary historical sources, the *Life of St Oswald*, and *The Battle of Maldon*, a famous, though incomplete, Anglo-Saxon poem.

Set off along the river wall for the five-mile-plus walk to Maylandsea. Opposite is Northey Island.

> Northey Island - where the Viking army mustered before the battle - is a Nature Reserve connected to the mainland by a causeway accessible at low tide. Acquired by the National Trust it provides a quiet haven for wildlife in an otherwise busy estuary. It is important in winter months as a secure feeding ground for about 3,000 Brent Geese who later breed on the Russian tundra. In summer when the estuary is most heavily used for all kinds of water sports, the island provides both a quiet breeding site and high tide roost for many wading birds when they have nowhere else to land.

It is possible to make a circuit of Limbourne Creek, commencing on your right, but you keep straight on. However, later, as you commence passing the delightful island of Osea over on your left, you must follow the wall round Cooper's Creek.

> In 1916 Osea Island became a Royal Navy secret base for motor torpedo

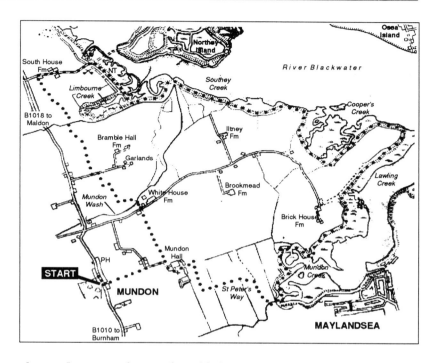

boats. It remained a naval establishment until 1926. It is linked to the mainland by a causeway only accessible at low tide. The enviably-sited mansion which you see was built in 1910.

A short distance after returning to the main river you turn right for good to follow Lawling Creek towards Maylandsea. It seems to take forever and the wall snakes its way around every little bend and inlet, finally reaching the boats at Mundon Creek. As you make the final turn towards the end of the row of houses at Maylandsea you negotiate a double width stile and instead come down the bank on your right, passing a metal gate to head away from the creek.

Set off beside a barbed wire fence and cross a new footbridge on your right by a waymark sign for St Peter's Way, a long distance footpath. Any thoughts that this would ensure an easy return to the start are quickly dashed as you head off again straight over a prairie-style cultivated field. On my visit the local farmer had cut a path through the head-high oil seed rape which took me to the centre of the field and then left to the end, but I cannot say how the way will look on your visit, although thse are roughly the directions you are looking for. After reaching the left hand side of this field cross a culvert and head straight over the next field as directed by the yellow waymark arrows, but only for a short distance. Now turn half right and head across the remainder of the field towards the farm buildings of Mundon Hall. Cross into a meadow full of old, dead oak trees, a strange sight, and leave by the gate at the top. (The official route, now in dispute, goes left and across the ancient moat via a bridge to reach the redundant church; however, with the bridge long since gone and too expensive to replace this is no longer possible. The owners of the hall appear quite happy for walkers to pass through the hall on the route we are taken but there appears to be a lack of progress with this being adopted officially). Over the gate, turn left and immediately left again to cross another and enter a grazing meadow. Cross diagonally to reach the church, now abandoned and well hidden in undergrowth.

> Mundon's Church of St Mary was declared redundant in 1970 and leased to the Friends of Friendless Churches in 1975. Isolated from the village but close to its hall, the design is strange with a remarkable timber tower standing only just above the nave roof, half an octagonal in shape fitting round the west wall and forming the belfry which contains, or contained, one of the oldest bells in the county. The church which, regrettably, is not open to visitors, has a Norman font, its oldest relic, and box pews.
> Just beyond the church, across its ancient moat which long pre-dates it, stands the present Mundon Hall.

Follow the metalled lane away from the hall and on to the bend by the pristine thatched cottage and large willow tree. Here you leave it to carry straight on along the stony track on which you set out back to the village and your starting point.

THE RIVER BLACKWATER & COAST
Walk 14: Bradwell-on-Sea

Start: *Bradwell-on-Sea is reached by taking the B1018 road from Maldon signposted to Burnham. Then the B1010 to Latchingdon, leaving it here to take the road to Mayland and Bradwell. Turn right to the village and right again at the junction in the High Street to park by the church.*

O.S.Maps: *Landranger 168; Pathfinder 1100 & 1123.*

Distance: *8 miles*

Refreshments: *The only refreshments available are in Bradwell itself where there are 2 pubs. The Bradwell Kings Head, opposite the church, provides food all day.*

Description: *One of the easiest both to walk and follow, you set off for Bradwell Waterside via a quiet road and a well-used field path. The 2½ mile walk along the sea wall spans 1,300 years of history from Bradwell Nuclear Power Station, begun in 1957, to St Peter-on-the-Wall Saxon Chapel of 654 A.D. You return by fields and quiet country lanes.*

WALK BACK OUT ON THE HIGH STREET opposite the Bradwell Kings Head and turn right. You leave the village and pass one road going off left to Latchingdon and Southminster and when you reach the next, cut over the junction and take the 'Wildside Walk' footpath over a shingle drive and running behind a row of properties. Fenced back gardens are to your left and, after a cluster of trees, a cultivated field commences on your right. The well-worn path then runs between open fields and continues diagonally through the next field. On the far side a path runs between properties to reach the road on a bend.
Carry straight on into Bradwell Waterside and turn left along a footpath by Quay House to bring you out at Bradwell Marina.

From 1850-1932 the Parkers, a local farming family, owned and sailed forty barges out of Bradwell Waterside. The dozen moorings here in 1960 had risen to 150 by 1993 with the popularity of leisure boating.

Turn right along the sea wall and right again to bring you back to the concrete roadway. Cross over and turn right, setting off along the sea wall again. On your right are static homes and across the water on your left, Pewet Island. Ahead looms Bradwell Nuclear Power Station.

A part of the marshes was filled in for the building of the nuclear power station in 1949, the baffle being built in the area where the sea bream and bass breed. The station, designed by Maurice Bibb, was begun in 1957 and commissioned in 1962; it is now one of the country's oldest.

Accompanied by the increasing and rather disconcerting hum of its machinery, you arrive opposite the power station by a beach.

The beach appears at first glance to be shingle but is, in fact, comprised entirely of shell! These are mostly cockle shells but several others can be found including mussel, oyster, whelk, periwinkle and limpet. The Blackwater Estuary is part of a Special Protection Area safeguarded under an EEC Directive on the Conservation of Wild Birds. It is also designated as a Ramsar Site under an International Convention to protect wetlands of international importance. The shore, sea wall and borrow dyke - down on your right - are all Sites of Special Scientific Interest and are part of the Dengie National Nature Reserve. You will not be surprised to learn that with such powerful and influential protection, by law, nothing can be removed from here!

In summer oystercatchers breed on the foreshore whilst black-headed gulls nest on the adjacent marshes. In winter, brent geese arrive from their arctic breeding grounds. On the shore, just above the high water level, is shrubby seablite, a locally common plant, but rare in Britain as a whole. On the sea wall itself are plants such as hoary cress and sea beet.

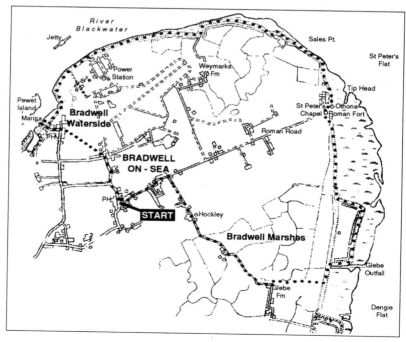

As you approach the headland you pass an area of salt marsh and at Sales Point an extensive area of mud flats.

A bombing range was established on the Dengie Mudflats in 1938. The row of lighters you can see strung out across the flats were sunk to try and stop coastal erosion from wave action. Across the water is the town of West Mersea on Mersea Island.

As you turn south you can pick out the isolated St Peter's Chapel on an elevated site in the distance ahead. You first pass the Othona Christian Community founded in 1946 to promote and provide a simple lifestyle of work, worship, study and play. Beyond their wooded settlement you come upon one of England's oldest and least known historic sites.

The little Chapel of St Peter-on-the-Wall, standing astride the west wall of the Roman Saxon Shore Fort of Othona, makes a moving sight. The fort dates back to the the 3rd century, and the only remains are of a 4 foot high fragment of south wall. However, excavations show that it was 520 feet long with walls 12 feet thick. The east walls have been destroyed by the sea and the north wall was at least 290 feet long. The chapel, one of the oldest in Britain, was built by Bishop Cedd around 654 A.D. What remains is the nave but there is evidence that it once had an apsed chancel and west porch. The church was almost entirely built of Roman stone and tile.

Return to the sea wall and carry on past the extensive mud flats at Gunners Creek and Bradwell Cockle Spit Nature Reserve managed by Essex Wildlife Trust. The wall makes a detour by turning left and running closer to the sea before returning to its original line at Glebe Outfall. Just after this look for a culvert across the water channel running parallel down on your right. At this point go down the bank, cross the water and head away from the wall across the open cultivated field, on a line just to the right of the barns of Glebe Farm. You cross another culvert and skirt a curved water course to the left before arriving on a track near the barn. Turn left and walk to the metalled country lane on a bend.
Turn right and follow Hockley Lane all the way back to Bradwell. You arrive at a T-junction opposite Dormer Cottage and turn left along a stretch of Roman road which runs to the Roman fort. Enter the village and arrive back at the church, your starting point, passing the village lock-up on the edge of the churchyard.

St Thomas's Church is mainly restored 14th and 15th century with an early 18th century brick west tower. The brick cage by the corner of the church-yard was the village lock-up for the temporary incarceration of local wrong-doers and has an attached whipping-post where on-the-spot justice was often carried out.

The River Chelmer at Little Baddow (Walk 17).

The River Chelmer

Choice Chelmer comes along, a Nymph most neatly clear,
Which well-near through the midst doth cut the wealthy sheere.
By Dunmow gliding down to Chelmsford holds her chase,
To which she gives the name, which as she doth embrace
Clear Can comes tripping in, and doth with Chelmer close:
With whose supply (though small as yet) she greater grows.
She for old Maldon makes, where in her passing by,
She to remembrance calls that Roman colony.
When Chelmer scarce arrives in her most wish'd bay,
But Blackwater comes in, through many a crooked way,
Which Pant was called of yore; but that, by Time exiled,
She Freshwell after hight, then Blackwater instyled.

(Polyolbion 1622 - Michael Drayton)

THE CHELMER is 35 miles long and rises in Rowney Wood in the parish of Debden. It was canalised in 1793 from the village of Springfield (now incorporated into Chelmsford) to the Blackwater estuary at Colliers Reach, off Heybridge to form the Chelmer & Blackwater Navigation. The waterway incorporated eleven locks to enable the ever increasing goods and materials demanded by the expanding population of the county town and its surrounding area to reach the sea-going vessels by-passing the port of Maldon. Not surprisingly Maldon, fully aware of the implications, fought long and hard to quash the various schemes put forward but in 1793, an Act of Parliament finally gave the go-ahead. In 1842, at the height of its prosperity, a remarkable total of 60,000 tons of cargo was carried up and down the canal. Ironically, much of this was for the construction of the railway which was to seal its fate.

Today it serves a fresh purpose with 36% of the water supplied by Essex & Suffolk Water being drawn from the Chelmer and Blackwater.

The quiet upper reaches are populated by chub and dace, while roach, pike, perch and, in small numbers, brown trout, inhabit the deeper sections.

THE RIVER CHELMER
Walk 15: Thaxted to Tilty

Start: *Take the B184 south from Saffron Walden or north from Great Dunmow; the B1051 from Bishop Stortford or the B1054 and B1051 from Halstead. Park near the Thaxted Pottery & Crafts just along the B184 road to Great Dunmow on the southern edge of town. (You may get permission to use their car park).*

O.S.Maps: *Landranger 167; Pathfinder 1051 & 1075.*

Distance: *7 miles*

Refreshments: *There is a good choice of refreshment opportunities in Thaxted but only one pub situated just off the walk itself, at Monk Street. Thaxted Pottery & Crafts have a tea room serving a range of light snacks; the pottery and craft shop is well worth a browse.*

Description: *The walk begins dramatically, then proceeds along quiet tracks and field paths to reach the tributary of the River Chelmer near The Breach Farm, which you follow to reach the main river at Tilty. After visiting the abbey remains you follow the bank of the youthful Chelmer for over 2 miles along the Harcamlow Way, a long distance footpath.*

FROM THE CRAFT CENTRE turn left along the B184 for a few yards before crossing and heading up a wide grass track (ANOTHER POSSIBLE PARKING SPOT) bearing right by a post and rail fence. Cross another track and turn right to commence one of the most dramatic starts to any East Anglian walk. The wide inviting grassy track drops down the valley and heads up the far side, creating stunning views across the Roman road, the B184, over on your right and back to Thaxted Church and windmill. Go over a cross-track and continue on between open fields and then along a path with a hedge commencing on your right. Switch to the right side of the hedge and the left side of the field on your left and, just before the end, cross a plank bridge over the ditch and carry on with a hedge on your left for 120 yards before turning right on a grass path running between open fields. At Richmond's Farm ignore the yellow waymark left and carry straight on between farm buildings, then turn right to reach a quiet country road at Richmond's Green. Turn right and pass Greenways on the bend and turn left over a concrete hardstanding to pick up a wide grassy track beside a field. Entering the next field you come to a crossways of green tracks and turn right along a short length of green lane passing the odd dilapidated barn. The way becomes metalled as you enter Sibley's Green and pass the farm and a scattering of detached properties. Immediately past the house on the left follow the footpath sign left along a concrete track. Later, when it bends left at the trees, go ahead through a gap into a cultivated field. Head straight over on a cleared path aiming for a point between an oak tree

and an exposed telegraph pole in the field corner where you join a lovely shady green lane. You come out on a country lane which you cross to walk down the left side of the garden of a house via a gap in the hedge by a telegraph pole.
Come out on to a cultivated field. Unfortunately the route is straight over. (Sorry about this but we have to accept that this is often the norm, whilst the pleasant green lane we have just walked is now the exception.) Head towards a collection of telegraph poles which, as we approach, we find to be a line of poles which we can follow to the end of the field. Here you find a cart-track over a tributary of the River Chelmer. This is the furthest point of the walk. Turn right without crossing the bridge to follow the right bank of the stream which flows through quite a deep gull. Cross a dry ditch and carry on to the end of the next field. (The number of aircraft making their approach to nearby Stanstead makes you appreciate how the business being attracted to London's third airport has grown recently.) Go a few steps right to cross a culvert and carry on, the stream now flowing through light woodland. A plank bridge at the end of this field leads you through a 'nettley' section to reach a cross-track. Turn left to join it for a few yards before turning right to follow the right bank of the stream, along the left side of a cultivated field as it winds its way slowly right to reach the road at a T-junction

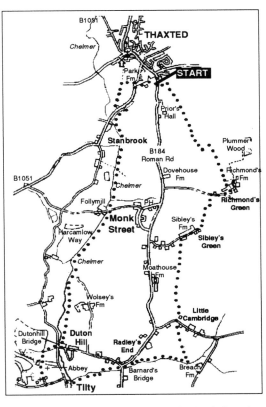

via a black British Gas maintenance hut at Radley's End, a part of the little hamlet of Duton Hill.
Go a few yards left and cross the road to take the footpath opposite by Barnard's Bridge. The wide grass path runs beside a plantation of young trees. At the end go over a plank bridge along an overgrown path beside the stream with a fence on your right with, beyond it, large ornamental ponds complete with ducks and geese. (This path needs a few more walkers!) Through a clump of bushes and over a plank

bridge takes you to the corner of a cultivated field. Continue along the left side by the stream for a few yards before crossing a substantial footbridge and turning right to follow the left bank through a meadow. At the next hedge the plank footbridge appears to have collapsed to the bottom of the ditch, but luckily it's dry. Carry on through the next field and at the end cross an even more impressive footbridge at a point where your stream meets and joins the River Chelmer, here still in its infancy. Head diagonally over the meadow to a green gate where you cross a stile to reach a country lane by a T-junction.

Take the lane to Tilty and later turn right to reach the church and after a visit, carry on through a kissing gate and down the meadow ahead to see the sparse remains of the Norman abbey over to your right.

> The nave of St Mary The Virgin, now the parish church, was built in 1220 as a little chapel to the nearby abbey. The East wall of its lovely chancel, added in the 14th century, is almost filled by a massive window with fine tracery. 14th century roof timbers which connected the nave and chancel are hidden beneath plaster. One of the abbots is remembered in brass and there are other Tudor brasses to Gerald Danet and George Medeley.
>
> The Cistercian Abbey, of which only fragments of the East wall of the cellarer's range remain, was founded here in the Chelmer valley in 1153. Excavations have shown there was once an abbey church with a chapter house and other buildings.

Leave the meadow by a single wooden gate by the dilapidated mill.

> Tilty Mill was built around 1750, possibly on the site of, and a conversion from an earlier timber mill. Although only a tiny tributary of the Chelmer passes here, it had been specially widened and deepened to provide a sufficient head of water to drive the wheel. The mill had ceased grinding long before the last war but until 1957 the owner had processed his cattle food by linking the water wheel to a hammer-mill. Now boarded up and abandoned, it is being overtaken by nettles and brambles, its machinery silent and rusting.

Walk along the farm track past an open straw barn and round a metal farm gate to carry on along the right side of an old meadow. At the trees join a well-used path coming in from the left and after crossing the stream by a little brick bridge, turn right to follow its left bank to the road. This is Harcamlow Way, a long distance footpath which you will follow almost back to Thaxted. Cross the T-junction at Duton Hill and Dutonhill Bridge carrying the road over the River Chelmer. Look for a footpath sign in the fence on the left where you cross the lawns in front of a bungalow and join the bank of the river. Go through an opening in the hedge at the end of the lawn and set off to follow the river bank for over two miles.

Shortly your way is barred by a hedge and you will need to turn right and go round and cut diagonally across the rough grass back to the bank with an unusually hilly landscape to your right. Wolsey's Farm is over to your right and then Brick House Farm across the river on your left. Later you pass a cart bridge, the first river crossing since the road. You pass another and, at the end of the field, go over a stile into a grazing meadow. Beyond it cross two further stiles to reach Folly Mill Lane. Follymill itself is to your left by the bridge.

Cross over, and a few steps to the left, go over a stile and return to the river bank. Walk by grazing meadows then over a stile and plank bridge to continue along the left side of a meadow. Another stile leads you by a cultivated field. Ignore a cross path leading via a footbridge over the river and carry straight on. Your way gets wider and firmer and round the bend the church spire and windmill back at Thaxted appear ahead. Meet a track and bear left to stay with the river for a short distance before it runs on under the road bridge and you leave it to bear right with the track running parallel with the road and a stream on your left. When you reach a footbridge with handrails cross the stream to reach the road.

Walk back down the road along the footpath and when it ends cross to the far side and carry on to just past the entrance gates of a house. Locate a footpath sign and turn right here skirting the garden and continuing along the right side of a field. Then continue on a wide grassy track between open fields, the church spire and windmill looming ahead. At the end of the field on your left you meet a cross track. The route is right towards the buildings of Park Farm. Keep bearing right as you enter the farmyard to exit on the road on a bend. Cross over and turn right past Park Lodge and the end of the 30mph limit. Walk round the bend and turn off left on a footpath along the left side of a field with the rear grounds of properties on your left. Walk up the drive by a bungalow and along an enclosed, well-used path by the entrance to Thaxted Bowls Club. Reach the B184 and turn right past the Centre for the Physically Disabled and back to Thaxted Pottery & Crafts car park, your starting point, for a refreshment break and a browse.

Try to find time for a wander round Thaxted. The old town has a number of places of interest including the unique 15th century Guildhall with its open ground floor, and the St John the Baptist, one of the grandest churches in the county of almost cathedral proportions, 183 feet long, 87 feet wide and with a spire that reaches 181 feet. The interior holds delights in plenty including magnificent hammerbeam roofs and a font unique in England.

THE RIVER CHELMER
Walk 16: Felstead

Start: *Felstead is situated on the B1417 a few miles off the A120 midway between Braintree and Great Dunmow. Leave the B1417 at the point where it turns sharp left in the centre of town and carry on for a few yards and park in the free car park on the right in front of the church.*

O.S.Maps: *Landranger 167; Pathfinder 1075 & 1098.*

Distance: *8 miles*

Refreshments: *Felstead is surprisingly well endowed with pubs and restaurants but unfortunately there are no refreshment opportunities on the walk itself - rather ironically, as you pass Ridley's Brewery on the way - but if you're desperate you could make a short detour to the pub at Littley Green or the one at Ford End.*

Description: *The walk is divided into two sections; the first takes you out of Felstead and by paths, tracks and quiet country lanes to Littley Green where you join the River Chelmer. Here you have the option of an additional walk beside both banks before the return journey which is entirely along the left bank from Ridley's Brewery back to Felstead.*

COME OUT OF THE CAR PARK and turn left. Walk past the junction with the B1417 and cross over to carry on for some way passing the Swan, the Boathouse Restaurant and Rumbles Cottage Restaurant. Immediately past Follyfield House, a part of Felstead School, turn right along a path between a hedge and wooden fence to enter playing fields. Carry straight over and cross a culvert to reach a cultivated field. Turn left for a few paces and then right to head straight through the field on a clear path. On the far side turn left and at the end of the field meet a well-used cross path. A path continues ahead straight through an open field but you turn right, the path is at first enclosed by high hedges then follows the right side of a field with the hedge on your right.

You meet a firm farm track and turn left on to it but as it bends right you carry straight on between high hedges, on what develops into a grassy track passing the entrance gates leading to Jollyboys. Continue along the right side of a field, hedged on the right towards the buildings of Potash Farm. Pass the farm on a stony track leading to the road at the hamlet of Cobbler's Green.

Carry on along this quiet country road to reach Brook Cottage. At the end of the garden boundary leave the road by turning right and crossing a plank bridge to walk up the right side of a cultivated field. At the end of the field a metalled track crosses your path. Turn right on to it for a few yards before turning left along a wide grassy track. At a small lake, one of a series of fish ponds connected with Leez Priory, turn left and at the end of the water go over a concrete culvert and turn right to walk along the right side of a long rough meadow beside the river Ter on your right, here little more than a stream feeding the line of fish ponds. At the end go over a stile into another long meadow, this one fitted with jumps for horses. Head on through and just before the end go over a stile set in the fence on the right, followed by an old wooden cartbridge. Bear left and, keeping a fence on your right carry on to cross a plank bridge to join a lane close to a junction. Turn right and then left at the junction to reach the entrance to Leez Priory on a bend.

> Leez Priory, standing in the hamlet of Little Leighs on the river Ter, was founded for Augustinian Canons early in the 13th century. When it was dissolved in 1536 it was given to Henry VIII's Chancellor Lord Rich who pulled down most of it and built himself a mansion on the site. Here he kept Princess Elizabeth prisoner in the reign of Queen Mary. Most of this house was ignominiously pulled down by the governors of Guys Hospital, a later owner, in 1753 leaving a somewhat confusing mix of medieval and Tudor remains for the layman to identify. Nevertheless along with its fine gardens, it forms a quite charming picture. Both the priory and gardens are open to the public at certain times.

Follow the bend right and when the road bends sharp left, carry on along a firm metalled track heading straight as an arrow. Pass a concrete hardstanding and down to meet a country lane on an S bend by Littley Park. Continue on ahead along the lane and when it bears right and a farm track forks left down to a cart bridge crossing the River Chelmer, you have options.
You can save just over a mile by cutting out the trip left along the river bank and back by the far side, and carry on along the road from this point*, or, for the full walk, go round the metal farm gate and walk down to the bridge. Just prior to it, go over a stile on the left and pick up the river bank. Walk by the river through the meadow and, crossing another stile continue on, your progress broken by further stiles and plank bridges. The meadows end and you negotiate a stile set amidst hedges and trees, crossing a well-worn path beside a ford, up the bank and round to walk over a concrete footbridge with handrails spanning the river. This is the furthest point of your walk and a lovely spot to take a break listening to the water as it negotiates the pebbly river bed.
Walk round to the path by the ford and join it heading left between high hedges. At the pillbox, the first of several, turn right to carry on along the right side of a cultivated field, river now on your right. Continue through the fields dotted with pillboxes and via several plank bridges. When you come to a grazing meadow the correct route is along the left side away from the river, but I can't see any real objection if you wanted to stay by the bank, although you must leave the meadow by the stile at the far left corner. Turn right and walk back down the farm track to the metal gate which you round to arrive back on the road where you turn left*. You arrive at the junction with the B1417 opposite Ridley's Hartford End Brewery.

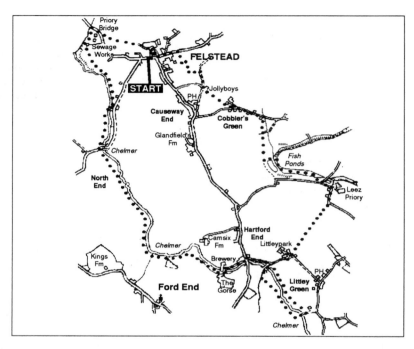

Turn left and just before the river bridge go right through the yard beside the brewery buildings.

The Brewery was built in 1842 by Thomas Ridley, eldest son of William Ridley, the miller, who lived and worked the nearby mill. Thomas saw the advantages to be gained from adding the brewery business to those of milling and malting. Its siting had gained the description of being "one of the most picturesque 'tower' breweries remaining in operation in England". The company still thrives, in 1988 it had 65 houses of its own and supplied beer to other tied and free houses.

Continue along the private road beyond which leads you to the mill.

The Ridley family had operated this mill since at least 1839 and it continued in production until around 1919. It finally closed in 1923. Stripped of its machinery, the mill along with the mill house has been converted to a charmingly-sited family residence.

Turn left and cross the bridge in front of the mill by the mill pond and go through a wooden gate into a rough meadow in front of woodland. Turn right and go over

a metal gate through wooded undergrowth past lockgates. Continue by the river along an overgrown path then on the right side of a narrow meadow. The path switches to the left side of the field away from the river and then cuts diagonally across back to meet the river bank just past a pillbox. The river loops right and, if convenient, you can keep straight ahead over the field to meet it again. You now settle down to follow the left bank of the river for nearly 2½ miles back to Felstead, you way interspersed by the odd footbridge and pillbox. The grass was thick and unattended on my visit during May and I was left with the feeling that no-one had passed this way before me; I hope this may have changed by the time of your visit. As you press on, the only sign of human habitation encountered are the cultivated fields through which the Chelmer shyly snakes its way. You pass a very rustic pillbox and eventually pass through undergrowth to cross a stile and arrive at Mill Road by the road bridge.

Cross over and negotiate the stile beyond to enter a long meadow with the river forming the right boundary. A wide grassy path runs round to the right and along the river bank via a weir and also round to the left along the hedge. Officially you should take that following the left side of the meadow, but either way you will end up by a metal gate at the far end in front of Felstead Mill (seen at its most scenic from the right hand side of the meadow).

> There has been a mill on this site since Domesday. In 1373 it was mentioned as belonging to nearby Leez Priory and had an earlier title of Abchild Mill. William Ridley owned it in 1848 in addition to his mill at Hartford End, but about 10 years later it was reported as having been burned down. It was rebuilt the next year and was still working up to around 1960.

Go through the gate and cut diagonally over to cross two footbridges beside the mill. Don't be put off by the fact that you are now in the garden of the mill; this is the right of way. Turn left and walk over to a stile close by the bank. Pass through the rear of another garden skirting to the right of an air-raid shelter, and going through a wooden gate to head away along the left side of a field with the Chelmer beside you on the left. Halfway along a long meadow take a footpath left and right through rough grass beside a high bank on your left. At the end cross a track and head down to continue as before, the fence of a sewage works on your right. Bear right with the fence and, keeping it on your right, make your way through rough ground on a bearly discernable path with the river joining you again and rushing over a weir, to reach the road by Priory Bridge.

Turn right and walk along the footpath up the hill passing the Felstead sign, crossing over and taking the footpath, forking left as the road bears right. Go over the rough grass and pick up a path following the left side of a cultivated field with Felstead Church straight ahead. At the end of the field go over two stiles on your left, crossing a track and another stile to walk along the right side of a new meadow. At the end go right over a stile to a concrete track. Turn right and pass Bury Farm, picking up a metalled drive and forking right in front of the house and right again before bearing left to exit the drive. Bearing right through a single wooden gate leads you back to the car park and your starting point. Beyond the car park, just before the road a drive goes right, serving properties and leading to the church entrance.

The Chelmer at Hartford End Mill.

The large body of the Church of Holy Cross is mainly of renewed 14th century but it has a Norman West tower and further 12th century work inside. There are also several 15th and 16th century monuments including a superb tomb to Lord Rich, Chancellor to Henry VIII (see Leez Priory) and his family, which adorn a special chapel he had built for the purpose. This is the work of Epiphanius Evesham, one of the first eminent English sculptors.

THE RIVER CHELMER
Walk 17: Little Baddow

Start: *From the A12 Colchester to Chelmsford road take the sliproad to Hatfield Peverel (B1137) and turn off to Little Baddow from the road to Boreham. Watch for a right turning into Holybread Lane by a post box. The church is about a mile along this lane on the right opposite Little Baddow Hall. Park in the layby.*

O.S.Maps: *Landranger 167; Pathfinder 1122.*

Distance: *9 miles*

Refreshments: *There is just the one pub in Little Baddow which is slightly off your route in the very early stages of the walk.*

Description: *The walk follows the tow path of the River Chelmer for over half its distance and the remainder comprises a mix of tracks, woodland and field paths, plus a few of the obligatory open field crossings. Much of the walk is along the Admiral McHardy Way created to commemorate 150 years of policing in Essex (1840-1990).*

LEAVE THE CHURCH on your left and walk the few yards before turning left by the house drive and bearing right by the open barn, to head away along a well-worn path by the right side of a field. Go over a footbridge in the corner and walk straight over the next field. You reach a stony track and turn right along it for about 175 yards towards the buildings of Holybreds Farm, before turning left over a plank bridge and across an open field towards the wood. Enter the trees and keep straight on. At a crossways of footpaths turn right and carry on this pleasant woodland path to reach the road.

Turn left and walk back along Holybread Lane to the staggered junction. Cross North Hill and take Tofts Chase opposite. The road climbs and just beyond the end of the brick wall on your right take the footpath sign right, then bearing left between holly hedges and mature oak trees. Go through the rough grass and over a plank bridge to cross a drive, and a stile beside a metal gate. Continue ahead on a wide grassy way between oaks still roughly parallel with the road, with horse grazing meadows either side. Go over a stile to reach a cultivated field. Cross straight over the grass and field beyond to meet a track.

Turn left and walk the few yards back to a fork. Turn right and head along the paved drive with 'sleeping policemen' to pass by the entrance gates to The Coach House. Continue past the wall on to a dirt track and when it bears right leave it to walk along the left side of the cultivated field to your right for a few yards. Go over a footbridge on your left and cross straight down the open field towards the wood which you enter via another footbridge, to enjoy another section of woodland path. Pass a clearing and climb to a stile. Carry on and leave by another stile to enter a rough meadow. Walk straight on to the end where a stile leads you to Tofts Chase, a country lane, where you turn left. Follow the bend left and down the hill. At the bottom take the concrete drive on the right. When it turns left towards Bassett's Farm, carry straight on through a gateway. The track bends right winding through a rough meadow. Bearing left the stony track ends and you continue along the right side of a meadow used for turf cutting to reach the river by an arched metal footbridge with white handrails. Do not cross the bridge but instead turn left along the tow path of the **Chelmer & Blackwater Canal.**

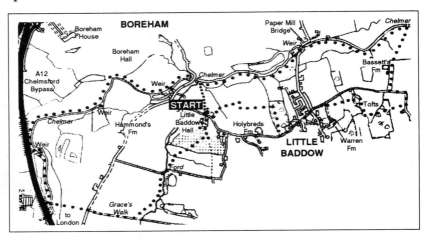

By the early eighteenth century it became obvious to the traders of the county town of Chelmsford, suffering from costly delays in moving goods along the winding, unmade Essex roads to the port at Maldon with its coastal trading ships, that a direct link to the sea would prove commercially beneficial. The idea of a canal using the combined forces of the River Chelmer and the Blackwater Estuary was mooted as early as 1677, but due to costs and the not unexpected objections from Maldon, it took until 1793 to get the scheme finally off the ground. Problems with Maldon were avoided by terminating the canal at Colliers Reach, off Heybridge, just short of the town. At the height of its prosperity in 1842, a year before the railway reached Chelmsford, The Chelmer & Blackwater Navigation carried a remarkable 60,000 tons of cargo up and down the canal - ironically much of it for the construction of the railway which would ultimately make it redundant!

You eventually reach a road and cross Paper Mill Bridge to arrive at the colourful scene of Paper Mill Lock.

In 1792 a pair of mills stood on an island just below the lock here grinding corn and pulping rags to make paper - the first place in Essex to produce paper. The last mill burnt down in 1905 ending a milling industry on the site going back to at least 1338. The Navigation Company set up stables here so that bargeees and their horses could receive refreshments and a night's rest. Moored here is the last barge to use the canal.

The Chelmer at Paper Mill Lock.

Carry on along the path and, just before the next road bridge, you have the opportunity to shorten your walk by turning left, crossing a stile just before a footbridge with blue handrails, and heading straight up the open field back to Little Baddow Church sitting prominently on the hill.

The full walk continues over the footbridge and along **Admiral McHardy Way**, which commemorates 150 years of policing in Essex (1840-1990). Cross **Boreham Bridge** and switch to the right bank where Sandon Brook joins the Chelmer.

At the point where Boreham Brook comes in to add its waters you pass the lovely Little Baddow Mill Lock, also known as King's Lock where the large mill pool fronts two waterfalls. The mill, which had been rebuilt only twenty years before the canal opened, was burnt to the ground in 1892, a fate which was to befall so many. A house now stands on the site.

The river now bears right and then makes a sharp turn left to arrive at Stonehams, another beautifully maintained working lock and weir. As the path bends right again you can no longer avoid the mesmerising sight and increasing sound generated by the A12, the busiest artery connecting East Anglia with London. This elevated section which bypasses Chelmsford provides a powerful reminder of the manic speed we are all inclined to take for granted harnessed to the performance offered by even the most modest of today's motors. The Chelmer now runs parallel with the road passing through Cuton, another delightful lock. Just before the river bears right to pass under the road you cross it by an impressive metal footbridge. Walk straight over the open field to a less pretentious footbridge with just a tiny stream to span. Head up the next field passing to the left of the pylon to reach a road. Cross straight over and enter Gracie's Lane, a stony track which runs straight and true for over a mile.

The lane running between an avenue of trees once led to Graces, the 16th century home of Henry Mildmay who fought in Ireland and died in 1639.

You only follow it for half this distance just to the bottom of the valley where you take the footpath left which follows the right side of a field just before the track crosses Boreham Brook. At the end of the field go over a stile bearing left through rough grass and bushes. Pick up a well-used path running along the right side of a lovely old meadow, parallel with the brook, at first hidden by bushes. This is Waterhall Meadows, a nature reserve managed by the Essex Wildlife Trust. The meadow narrows down to a grassy track which leads to a stile, bringing you out to a little country lane beside a spectacular ford; a delightful spot to take a short break. Climb the bank on the far side of the lane and turn right to cross the footbridge beside the ford. Beyond cross the stile on the left and head diagonally right up the open field on a clearly-defined path. Go over a plank bridge spanning a ditch on the far side and continue over the next open field on the same line. On the far side head between fruit trees to pick up a stony track over on the right and turn left along it. Stay with the track as it bends left but when it bears right keep on ahead across the grass for a few yards before turning right between buildings to pick up the drive again as it heads towards the hall with the church tower beyond. Pass Little Baddow Hall and go over the stile beside the wooden gate out into the road opposite the church, your starting point.

The lovely timber-framed Hall dates from the 14th or 15th century.
St Mary the Virgin has a Norman nave and 14th century West tower. There is a fine tomb-chest featuring two oak effigies of a man and woman of c1320. There is also a monument to Henry Mildmay who died in 1639.

THE RIVER CHELMER
Walk 18: Woodham Walter, Langford & Maldon

Start: Take the road signposted right to Woodham Walter off the B1019 to Maldon, just south-east of Hatfield Peveral. Come into the village and park in the area of the church which you come to on the left.

O.S.Maps: Landranger 167 & 168; Pathfinder 1122 & 1123.

Distance: 10 miles

Refreshments: The Queen Victoria in Woodham Walter, a short distance from the start, and another on the northern outskirts of the village are your only refreshment opportunities on this relatively long walk, so it's best to carry some with you.

Description: There are basically two separate aspects to the walk. The journey to and from the River Chelmer consisting of tracks, minor country lanes, field paths and open field crossings, and the walk along the tow path of the river itself. In the case of the field crossings, they are all straight forward and most are on well-defined paths through the crops. A highlight of the walk is the point where a confusing configuration of water courses, weirs, locks and a system of sluices allow the Chelmer and Blackwater to join and form the Chelmer & Blackwater Navigation Canal.

GO THROUGH THE SINGLE wooden gate into the churchyard and pass along the left side to leave on the far side via a kissing gate - you can visit the church later. Cross straight over between the fields ahead on a grass path between the crops. At the end of the field on your left enter the wood over a plank bridge spanning a fast flowing brook. After a few yards meet a cross-path and turn left. After snaking its way for some distance it bears right to head away from the wood on a wide grassy path along the left side of a field with the worked-out grass-covered remains of gravel pits on your left. After passing a storage tank on a brick plinth you come to the end of the field and turn left on a stony farm track. The track swings right and left to pass between large derelict buildings on the right and the shell of a modest farmhouse on the left in a similar condition. Head away from this scene of desolation along the drive to meet a country road at a junction.

Cross straight over to take the metalled lane passing Waggers Country Kennels & Cattery. The lane ends at a T-junction where you turn right passing Guys Farm House. Look for an opening in the hedge on the left to take a path running along the left side of a cultivated field beside the boundary fence of the farmhouse grounds. When the boundary fence ends continue ahead through the open field on a well-defined path. On the far side continue by the hedge, and at the end of the field cross the shingle drive to Woodlands and carry on beside their boundary fence. When this ends move over to the track appearing on your left and carry on along this bearing left through the trees at a point where it forks right. There are fine views now of the Chelmer Valley over to your left. After veering right to cross a ditch on a wide grass culvert, the track peters out into a path running along the left side of a cultivated field still keeping on in the same direction as before. At the end of the field the path continues between open fields passing a single oak tree to reach a stony track.

Turn left along it for about 60 yards before turning right to cross a culvert by an oak tree and head straight through a field on a well-defined path. Cross a grass culvert and continue now along the left side of a field on a grassy path.

The walk has been very peaceful and devoid of both people and traffic, but the sounds of both begin to invade your privacy from here on as you approach Maldon and its bypass. However, just to balance things, this also means that the delights of the river walk are fast approaching. At the end of the field you reach a country lane and turn right. After a short distance turn left along the tree-lined drive to Beeleigh Abbey, now a private house. High manicured laurel hedges flank the entrance to this lovely old house and the peacock, which sat regally preening itself on the garden wall on my visit, completed a memorable picture.

> Beeleigh Abbey was founded about 1180 for Premonstratensian canons. In the 13th century remains, which included the Chapter House and the undercroft of the Dormitory, a lovely timbered house was built in the 16th century. This was home for many years to the Foyles, the famous London bookshop family. In the old dormitory, William Foyle housed his wonderful personal library. The whole effect is wonderfully satisfying.

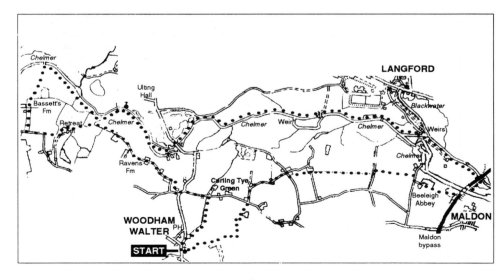

Pass through the gateway ahead and carry on along a path between old hedges. Go over a stile - your first of the walk - and enter a long narrow meadow. Views of the Chelmer and the new bridge over the river carrying the bypass appear to your left. Another stile leads you out along a well-used shady path between high hedges. You come out at the road bridge where you negotiate a stile and cross the busy road with care. Turn left and walk over the bridge, then right, down concrete steps on the far side. Turn immediately left at the bottom to take a grassy path running parallel with the road above, leading you to the banks of, not the River Chelmer, but the River Blackwater!

Turn left along the tow path passing under the bypass and by a lock. Pass a brick bridge over the river on your right and the golf course and its club house on your left. As you continue along the metalled drive by the course, the Chelmer converges from the left and, after you leave the drive which bears right to be taken over the river by another brick bridge, joins you and the Blackwater in a confused mass of water courses, weirs, locks, sluices and bridges. Let Stan Jarvis sort it out for us as we find a convenient vantage point amidst the milling waters; if the rivers have been swollen by recent rain, you'll find the vista even more exciting!

As Stan pointedly remarks in his excellent and very comprehensive book 'The Rivers Chelmer & Blackwater': 'The complicated flow of these waters, the Chelmer, the canal, the Blackwater, the Langford Cut and the tidal lagoon, once known as Beeleigh Harbour, has to be seen to be understood.' He explains: 'Opposite the mill at Langford, the river Blackwater on the west and the Langford Cut on the east meet at the junction of the Blackwater with the canal. In a complicated triangle of watercourses the canal runs on through a lock with one of the original brick-arched bridges above it, and heads on in a dead straight line to a point just west of Black Bridge in Heybridge where it reaches the tidal estuary of the Blackwater at Heybridge Basin.' Are you with him so far? He goes on: At the same triangle, through a system of sluices, the Chelmer is released from its bondage as a canal, passes the former mill at Beeleigh Falls and runs into the tidal waters of the estuary. The Blackwater, which now produces the flow for the canal, joins it here at Beeleigh Falls, where its surplus water is shed over the weir. This stream flows on to the estuary so the two rivers make Beeleigh Falls House an island.'

I hope that it's all clear to you now as I may ask questions later! Seriously, just enjoy the scene.

The next problem is how to get out. It's easier than it seems, though less obvious. Cross the footbridge over the weir and, at the lock gates, turn right and cross the footbridge with blue-painted metal handrails. Now turn left and set off along the right bank of the Chelmer. You pass a bridge carrying a large pipe across the river and, on your right, a large pumping station.

The huge pipe which bridges both canal and towpath - you'll pass another further on - carries water from the Chelmer and Blackwater Navigation to be treated at the waterworks here before being sent on to Hanningfield Reservoir. An estimated 35 million gallons goes daily to provide for the population of south and east Essex.

At the next brick bridge and lock gate, a tributary feeds off. Later you pass a deep weir and then the path swings right and then left to pass under a crude metal bridge carrying further pipes and then in front of properties at Sugar Baker's Holes, the first sign of human habitation for some way.

These are all that remains of cottages built for the workers at Marriage, Reid & Marriage's who first commercially refined sugar in Britain in their sugar mill here in Ulting Lane in 1832 The process proved uncompetitive against the import of sugar cane and the enterprise was abandoned and the mill and most of the cottages demolished. Ironically, the Second World War saw the industry revive when home grown sugar became a vital need.

The path is now wooded and shady but, after passing over a footbridge, returns to its now familiar appearance. You reach your first and only road bridge where you cross the road and switch to the left bank to arrive at Hoe Mill Lock where a collection of brightly-coloured boats lie moored.

The headwaters and tail-race of Hoe Mill can still be detected though the mill was demolished in 1914. Over 13,000 sacks of flour were ground here and transported away on the canal in 1865.

Cross an impressive new footbridge by another weir and return to peace and the company of the odd moorhen. Quite suddenly the lovely little church at Ulting appears beside the river on the far bank - the only church along the course of the Chelmer which actually stands on its bank.

Surprisingly the little Church of All Saints is almost entirely 13th century with a little turret and spire from the 15th century. Altogether it is beautifully preserved and totally enchanting.

You pass another lock - this one was being operated for a barge on my visit - and finally arrive at a concrete arched footbridge with white metal handrails. Here you leave the river path (which you can follow for another four miles on Walk 17) and turn left to walk the left side of a meadow used for turf cutting. At the end a rough track develops and you follow it, bearing right and left through a rough meadow to reach a concrete drive which leads you to a country lane, climbing steadily. Turn left along Tofts Chase and continue to climb up to the bend - quite a strain

on the legs at this late stage of the walk. There are again fine views of the Chelmer Valley and you will note that virtually all settlement has taken place well above the valley.

Leave the lane by carrying straight on over a cultivated field towards the buildings of Retreat Farm. You reach a stony track and turn left. Walk through the farm between buildings passing right of a grass 'roundabout' and left of a barn. Turn right along the meadow walking parallel with the river valley, and at the end cross a grass culvert. Turn left to walk along the edge of a field on a rough grass track now heading down towards the river. At the end of the field follow the boundary right as it takes an irregular course beside light woodland. Carry on along the right side of the next field gradually bearing away from the river over on your left but not before a last look across to the little church at Ulting passed earlier. Walk on past a wood on your right divided by a grassy ride. The track, turning ever firmer and more permanent, bears right and then climbs steeply left towards Raven's Farm.

The track becomes a shingle drive as you pass the delightful timber-framed farmhouse with its massive chimney stack strangely sited on the front of the house, and then a metalled lane bearing right. At the end of the garden boundary of the last property on the right, by a right-hand bend, look for a footpath sign partly hidden in the hedge, leading you straight on through a wooden gate and along a fenced path. Turn right between lines of fruit trees as directed by the yellow waymark arrows and go over a stile and between a house wall and a white pailing fence to come out on to the lane by a stile beside the drive.

Turn left and walk the few yards to the road junction. Cross over and turn left along the footpath and then right towards Curling Tye Green. At the end of the metalled footpath drop down the bank and carry on down to the road bridge between high hedges. Here, cross the stream and turn right by the footpath sign along a path bordered by a wire fence to your left, and a steep bank down to the stream on your right. Enter an area of woodland, and when you reach a partial clearing dotted with trees do not continue on the indistinct path which climbs ahead but instead, bear right along a clear path which then divides, both leading to similar footbridges sited close together. Take the one on the left and pass through an area of light woodland crossing duckboards bridging a damp, marshy section. Negotiate a rustic stile to break out of the trees and continue along the right side of a cultivated field. At the road turn left to head back up to the church, your starting point. (Note: a short distance right is the Bell Inn).

St Michael's Church is unusual in that it was rebuilt entirely in Elizabethan red brick in 1563. Roofed in tiles of the same colour, the overall effect is quite startling. Some things have been saved from its medieval origins, however, notably the font, while there is medieval glass in several of the windows.

The timber-framed Bell Inn is also Elizabethan.

The River Crouch at South Woodham Ferrers (Walk 19)

The River Crouch

The Crouch is rising;
The twisting mirror channels swell with sky
Across the salting grass
And wires are hanging weed against the flooding tide.
Across the race Canewdon Church tower marks
A dome where stubble fields turn pale in failing light
And Hockley Woods hang silent as a shroud
Upon their dying ridge.

(North Fambridge - Barry Norrington)

THE RIVER CROUCH runs west to east, rises from three headstreams which come together just above Noak Bridge on the A176. It is 29 miles in length with the islands of Wallasea and Foulness forming its southern bank during the latter stages of its 19 tidal miles to the sea.

The only commercial navigation on the river today is that for the importation of timber to Wallasea Island - often by Russian vessels - but the Crouch still has a small shell fish industry and is renowned for its sailing facilities, particularly at Burnham.

The river has historic associations with The Battle of Ashingdon, fought on its southern shore at Ashingdon and Canewdon in 1016 between the Saxons under Edmund Ironside and the Danes led by King Cnut (Canute). Legend has it that it was on the northern shore in the little hamlet of Creaksea that he tried to hold back the tide, though there are other claimants for this famous site.

THE RIVER CROUCH
Walk 19: South Woodham Ferrers

Start: *On entering South Woodham Ferrers follow the ring road until you see brown signs to the Country Park and Open Farm. You will eventually turn along Marsh Farm Road. Pass the Country Park and its car park on the left and continue on to the river ford where you can park in the Country Park car park on the right.*

O.S.Maps: *Landranger 168; Pathfinder 1143*

Distance: *5½ miles*

Refreshments: *You may be able to obtain refreshments at the Country Park otherwise there are no opportunities on this relatively short walk. If you can cross the ford there is a pub just across the river at Hullbridge otherwise a short drive will bring you into the town centre.*

Description: *The continuing development of South Woodham Ferrers has resulted in new housing encroaching on areas that were once open and criss-crossed with footpaths. To save walking some distance through housing estates I have shortened the walk to comprise Fenn Creek and Hawbush and Clementsgreen Creeks. These are connected by the Marsh Farm Country Park, but if you are happy to make a linear walk, retracing your steps, there are opportunities here for further miles east along the sea wall of the Crouch, by the north bank of Clementsgreen Creek and the west bank of Stow Creek.*

SET OFF FROM THE CAR PARK by turning right along the bank of the Crouch and later bear right along Fenn Creek. You reach a point where a yellow waymark arrow sends you down the bank, through a gate and along a wide grassy track. You eventually reach the approach road to the ford via another gate and, crossing straight over, enter the car park to Marsh Farm Country Park.

Walk through the car park and between buildings. You will find toilets here (and possibly light refreshments). Carry on making your way right through to pick up a concrete track which leads away between grazing meadows to reach the sea wall, and a wooden gate and fence notifying you that this is a nature reserve.

Climb the bank overlooking Clementsgreen Creek and turn left for a short circuit of a section of the creek which, beyond the sluice gates, is now kept dry apart from a narrow water course running down the centre. At the end of the water on your right, turn right and pass over the sluice to circle the dry northern section of the creek anti-clockwise.

The mounds are remains of medieval salt workings remembered in Saltcoates, the house situated between the end of the creek and the railway.

Return to the sluice and retrace your steps back to the wooden gate by the nature reserve notice board. This time carry on along the sea wall passing Hawbush Creek with Clementsgreen Creek beyond.

A jetty here was used to transport bricks from the Woodham Ferris Brick Company between 1898 and 1908.

Round the point at the end of the Creek you arrive at the main river Crouch at Brandyhole Reach. The river then widens into Brandy Hole.

This intriguing name resulted from innovative 18th century smugglers' habit of sinking their contraband brandy attached to blocks of salt when chased by the Revenue men. When the danger had passed and the salt dissolved the brandy popped back up to the surface to be retrieved!

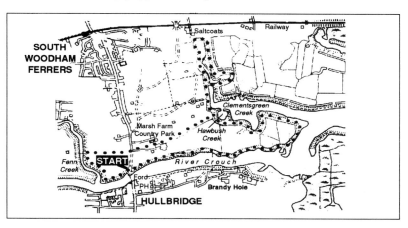

You pass the small development of Brandy Hole now comprising mostly of caravans. Slipways and a landing stage service the increasing number of yachts and small boats now liberally scattered across the river as you approach the ford linking Hullbridge on the far shore with the car park, your starting point.

Remains of a medieval bridge, which fell down in 1769, remained at Hullbridge until 1930 and was replaced by Battle Bridge at the head of the tidal water. At one time barge wharves also lined both banks and a rowing ferry formed a regular link until 1948.

THE RIVER CROUCH
Walk 20: Burnham on Crouch & Creaksea

Start:	*Drive into Burnham town centre and park in the free car park in Ship Road (left opposite the clock tower).*
O.S.Maps:	*Landranger 168; Pathfinder 1143*
Distance:	*7 miles*
Refreshments:	*There are plenty of pubs, cafes and restaurants in Burnham but none on the walk beyond the town centre. This should not cause a problem as the walk is not lengthy.*
Description:	*The walk is planned to present two contrasting aspects to the river Crouch. Commencing at the quay you head east along the sea wall soon leaving all river activity behind you with only the views across to the deserted Wallasea Island for company. The second part takes you by track and field path back to the outskirts of town, and after working your way through the residential roads, by field paths back to the river west of Burnham. In contrast your return along the Crouch is filled with colour and activity as you skirt the marina and pass boats at anchor and at sail along the river to arrive back at the quay with its range of yacht clubs and boating shops.*

AFTER PARKING YOUR CAR come back out on to the high street. Pevsner is rather dismissive concerning the merit of its buildings though I found this not an unattractive town, especially if yachting is your first love. Cross over and take the little lane to the right of the clock tower, built in 1877, to reach the quay. Turn left by the White Hart Hotel, passing notice boards advertising river trips on the Crouch and ferry trips to Wallasea Island, and the Anchor, with its inviting brick seats overlooking the harbour. (This would make a pleasant place to relax, drink in hand, after your walk). A line of chandlers' shops line the quay to service members of the various yacht clubs based here, and you pass the impressive white buildings of the largest, The Royal Corinthian Yacht Club, before the earthen sea wall leads you away past laid-up boats and static homes to the peaceful haven downstream. Before you do so, take a short break on one of the bench seats atop an old pill-box for a look back over the harbour.

The Hythe Quay was part of the old port of Maldon and a number of Thames sailing barges were originally used here for transporting cargo - a few still use the quay today. In 1272 the whole river Crouch was granted to the Manor of Burnham and it remained in private hands until the Crouch Harbour Authority was formed in 1974. In the 19th century the Burnham Oyster Company rented the river bed from the Lords of the Manor and it was their merchants who built many of the large houses in the town.

The club house of the Royal Corinthian Yacht Club, looking more like the forward staff quarters of a cross-channel ferry, was built on 38 concrete piles driven in the river bed in 1931; an early example of a style of building which became synonymous with the '30s in England and can be seen most typically in cinemas of the period.

Resume your walk, the far bank comprising the northern shore of Wallasea Island.

In the 1920s, Wallasea Island was used for yacht building and the ferry service which once took workers across from Burnham was re-instated from the Town Steps in 1993. The name Wallasea appears to have originated from Wall Fleet, the old name for the river. During the 1953 floods, all the islands on the Crouch were submerged.

The sea wall here is very high, protecting the low lands of the old Dengie Marshes to your left, now extensively farmed.

On the ancient shoreline of the marshes are Red Hills, created by Iron Age salt production. There were about 200 Red Hills in Essex, many of them here and along the Blackwater; most have been destroyed.

A short way beyond the metal stepless stile, come down the bank and take a track heading away from the river. When it bears right and becomes concrete surfaced, leave it by carrying straight on along a path by the left side of a cultivated field. At the end of the field bear left on a firm, wide farm track bearing right. The track then goes slowly left and becomes concrete. Cross Pannel's Brook by a hard-standing and pass under power lines. A footpath sign sends you right on a wide grassy strip with a plantation of young trees on your left, leaving the track which continues to Burnham Wick Farm ('Wick' is Anglo-Saxon for 'Dairy'). After about 200 yards pick up a well-worn path going left between open fields and passing a line of seven trees. At the end of the field the path goes left for 100 yards, then right along the right side of a grazing meadow with a hedge on your right. When the hedge ends, carry on between open fields, and at the cross-path turn left, still between open fields, to reach a private road on a bend.

Turn right along Wick Road, and just past a garage block and properties on your left, follow the road left and then right passing Silver Road on your left. You then pass Ship Road and your car park in Providence, where you could finish your walk - there's much more to see yet so ignore any temptation and carry on past. The road bears right and left and, just past Chapel Road, turn right into tree-lined Dorset Road. At the top turn left along Crouch Road which takes you to High Street by a post box.

Cross the road and take the enclosed footpath beside number 59. Cross straight over a close and continue straight on. Cross Fernlea Road and carry on along the footpath which comes out on an estate of modern detached houses. Look for a path on your left between houses which will bring you out on a large green area. Head for the seat and bearing slightly left continue along the faint grass path to cross the access road to Burnham Yacht Harbour. Continue through the grass, now parallel with the railway over on your right. At the end pick up a well-walked path heading along the right side of a cultivated field lined by poplars with a hedge between you and the railway on the right, and the Crouch appearing away over to the left. At the end of the field by the railway gates follow the field boundary left, passing Creaksea Place Farm buildings and heading for the river. The path bends left, passing through a clump of bushes to arrive by the sea wall at Creaksea.

> Legend has it that Creaksea is the site of the Danish King Cnut's (Canute) attempt to hold back the tide - the site of his battle with the Saxons is on the far side of the river between Canewdon and Ashingdon.

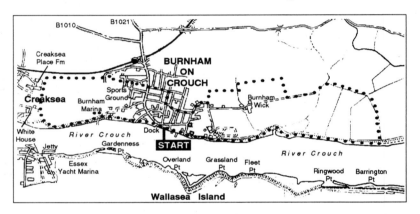

> Across the water, to the right, is the north-west corner of Wallasea Island by Lion Creek which has seen a certain amount of development. Timber is shipped from the jetty at the timber yard by quite large boats.

Set off back to Burnham to a more colourful and livelier river scene. You are diverted left round an inlet to skirt a large, colourful Marina before joining the attractive brick promenade back at the harbour. There are also further refreshment opportunities before you reach the Tourist Information board and toilets. A few more paces takes you past a lovely terrace of low houses, the central section occupied by the White Hart Hotel, your starting point.

THE RIVER CROUCH
Walk 21: Canewdon

Start: *Canewdon is best reached by taking the A130 from the Chelmsford bypass (A12). Just beyond the roundabout with the A132, turn left to Battle-bridge. Turn left to Hullbridge and keep straight on along this road following the signs to Canewdon. Just before the village turn left up to the hall and church. Park in front of the church.*

O.S.Maps: *Landranger 168; Pathfinder 1143*

Distance: *8½ miles*

Refreshments: *You pass The Anchor and The Chequers on your return to Canewdon, but there are no refreshment opportunities on the walk itself.*

Description: *An easy walk commencing with a breathtaking descent from the church, through fields with wonderful panoramic views, and across open fields to the river. There follows a walk of nearly 4 miles along the Crouch and up to Lion Creek. The return is almost entirely across open fields but, like the outward journey from the church to the river, unless the oilseed rape is at its worst, the paths are well-defined and waymarked. Unfortunately you are forced to take to the road for the final stretch back to the church but this is usually quite quiet.*

OPPOSITE THE CHURCH are two footpath signs; you take the well-defined path forking right through a large cultivated field, passing to the right of a telegraph pole. The descent down Beacon Hill is dramatic and the panoramic views spectacular.

The village gained its fame (and maybe its name, though this is disputed) for having provided the site, along with neighbouring Ashingdon, for Edmund Ironside's losing battle with the Danes under King Cnut at the Battle of Assandun (Ashingdon) in 1016. Legend states that the Danes won because they held the position at the top of Beacon Hill.

Cross a concrete track and take the right fork over a stile into a meadow. Walk diagonally through the rough grass towards farm buildings. Go over another stile by a metal gate and cross the concrete drive to Bolt Hall. Continue along the left side of a field and go left over a plank bridge to cross another section of the concrete drive. Carry on along the left side of the field beyond by a deep ditch. Part way along a waymark arrow sends you diagonally right, cutting off the field corner to reach the end of a hedge line. From this internal field corner continue following the line of the waymark diagonally over the remainder of the field towards silos and buildings. At the next internal field corner turn right and head straight over the field to a waymark arrow on a telegraph pole on the far side. As you pass it and cross an area of rough grass, look back up to the church from where you began. The church perched atop the aptly named Beacon Hill will provide just that for most of the walk.

Cross a plank bridge and head straight over another open field through a clear gap in the crops. Cross a footbridge over a length of water, after which a firm wide track converges from the left and you join it as it sweeps right and bears left to cross a causeway over a dyke. Negotiate steps straddling an electric fence and climb the sea wall. Go down the other side and over a stile to join the path beside the river Crouch.

> You join the river opposite the entrance to Bridgemarsh Creek at the point where Bridgemarsh Island commences. In the distance to the left beyond Longpole Reach are the Yachts at North Fambridge.

Turn right and set off, soon rounding Landsend Point by Shortpole Reach. The sweeping bay takes in first Raypits Reach and, after passing Upper Raypits Farm, Easter Reach.

> There was once a cottage and brick kiln on what is now flat and featureless Bridgemarsh Island, but about 1921 the river wall broke due to poor maintenance and flooded the island, drowning 600 sheep. After further major flooding in 1933 it was finally abandoned and turned over to the wildfowlers as a reserve. The former Althorne Creek oyster grounds,

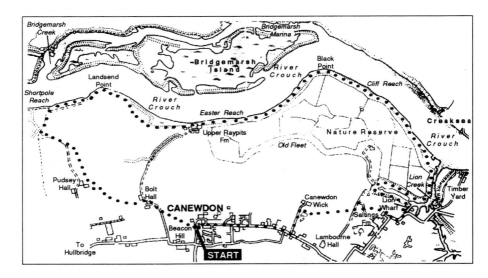

between the island and the far river bank, now provides a haven for the yachts of Bridgemarsh Marina, created here by floating pontoons in the river.

As you round Black Point, either on the sea wall which cuts off the point, or by the river on a grassy path, Bridgemarsh Island ends and you meet a stile at the entrance to Raypits Nature Reserve.

Lower Raypits, and Lion Creek which you reach shortly, are nature reserves managed and protected by the Essex Wildlife Trust. Covering nearly 160 acres and designated Sites of Special Scientific Interest by English Nature, they provide an important refuge for wintering geese and waders. The grazing marsh is one of the few unploughed marshes left on this part of the coast and as such is an important sanctuary for a whole range of wildlife adapted to the special conditions that exist here. The reserve was once part of an extensive saltings in the Crouch estuary but the saltmarsh was turned into pasture, criss-crossed with drainage ditches. The marshes were flooded in winter and the dykes would have always held water. The brackish conditions in the ditches and dykes and the salt in the soil now support a range of plants and animals.

The sea wall also supports many plants and animals including the rare Roesel's bush cricket, sea barley and grass vetchlings, with barn owls, short-eared owls and skylarks hunting and feeding overhead.

The open pasture provides grazing for large numbers of Brent geese in winter, nesting for skylarks and a refuge for small mammals and insects, while oystercatchers, dunlin, redshank and golden plover can be seen all year round.

The ditches and dykes help support many of the invertebrates such as dragon and damselflies, while reed bunting and sedge warblers nest among them.

The marshes are grazed and mown for the benefit of the grassland plants and the overwintering Brent geese. The sea wall is managed by cutting to provide the right habitat for insects and other invertebrates, which in time provide food for the birds and small mammals which hunt there.

Look out for adders which in hot weather sometimes bask on the sea wall; lapwings which breed on the wet pasture; dark-bellied Brent geese grazing on the pasture; short-eared owls hunting over the grassland in winter and skylarks, heard as well as seen through summer.

Now unobstructed by the flat and featureless island, the far bank now takes on a very pleasant aspect with little wooded hills rolling down to the foreshore, dotted with the occasional, idyllically situated property, up as far as the little hamlet of Creaksea, one of the the places nominated for the famous incident in legend where

King Cnut is said to have ordered back the tide.

You arrive at Lion Creek with the activity notably increasing on the river ahead as it approaches the major yachting centre of Burnham. The timber yard and jetty beyond the creek stands on Wallasea Island. Follow the sea wall right heading down this quiet length of water bordered by mudflats. The path then bears right to skirt a finger of water, returning to meet the end of the creek where it bears right by Lion Wharf to reach the road on a bend.

Turn right and follow the road as it bends right. When it bends sharp left, leave it to carry straight on over a metal stile beside a gate. Follow a wide grassy track for a short way, with saltings Poultry Farm over on your left, and when it ends, carry straight on through a field, passing to the left of a small group of trees. The path continues across the next open field bearing left. Cross a footbridge by a cross-track and continue over the next cultivated field. At the end cross a wide grass track and another, larger footbridge before walking diagonally over the next large field. A plank bridge enables you to cross the ditch beyond, and head through another, smaller field. Pick up the internal field corner and carry on along the left side to the end, passing a lovely lake with private fishing seen through the trees on your left - possibly the remains of former fish ponds - and Canewdon Wick farm on your right. Locate a stile in the field corner leading you to a shady green lane, at first a little overgrown, but later, after passing the entrance to the lake, wider and firmer. Arrive at Lambourne Hall Road and turn right to head back to Canewdon. You pass Gardiners Lane, and beyond Canewdon Village Hall, basic and very 60s-ish, eventually arriving at the High Street. When it bears left by The Anchor you carry straight on, passing The Chequers, to reach the church by the village lock-up. Enter the churchyard and beyond it, your starting point.

> The village lock-up situated at the entrance to the churchyard is dated 1775 and was restored in 1983. As it is thought that most villages provided similar confinement it is surprising that so few remain, although looking at the rather basic shed-like construction of this one perhaps it isn't! Inside is a set of original stocks.
>
> St Nicholas Church is not only impressively sited but massively, if rather crudely, constructed. Perhaps crude is a rather unkind description, but the grey ragstone blocks are hardly easy on the eye. Most of the church is 14th and 15th century and the bulky West tower, built in four stages, is 7 feet thick and rises to 75 feet. Inside is a wealth of carved wood and a font from the 13th century.

The River Roding & Cripsey Brook

It flows through flowery meads,
Gladdening the herds that on its margin brouse;
Its quiet bounty feeds
The alders that o'er shade it with their boughs.

Gently it murmurs by
The village churchyard, with a plaintive tone
Of dirge-like melody
For worth and beauty modest as its own.

More gaily now it sweeps
By the small schoolhouse, in the sunshine bright,
And o'er the pebbles leaps,
Like happy hearts by holiday made light.

(A Stream - Anon)

THE RODING rises at Molehill Green near Elsenham and flows for 45 miles to its confluence with the Thames at Barking Creek. It was made navigable for its last 3 miles from Ilford Bridge in 1764 (Ilford - 'ford over the river Hyle', 'Hyle' being the Roding's former name). Although it is shown on an Essex map to have had 5 mills along its banks in 1777, it now rarely attains full river status, appearing little more than a brook, especially when compared with the major waterways of the county. The Roding Valley does, however, provide the site for twenty-four churches.

Cripsey Brook is one of the Roding's two tributaries - the other being Seven Kings Water. It rises in Thornwood Common and joins the river at Ongar.

97

The River Roding at Fyfield (Walk 22).

THE RIVER RODING & CRIPSEY BROOK
Walk 22: Ongar, Moreton & Fyfield

Start:	*Just south of The Four Wantz roundabout at Ongar on the A414 from Chelmsford, turn off right along High Ongar Road and immediately left to park along the cul-de-sac.*
O.S.Maps:	*Landranger 167; Pathfinder 1121.*
Distance:	*6½ miles*
Refreshments:	*The only opportunity for refreshments outside Ongar appear to be The Queens Head, 150 yards off the route at Fyfield, so it would be best to travel prepared.*
Description:	*The walk follows the course of the Cripsey Brook through fields and meadows from Ongar to Moreton, then traverses the high farm land by track and field to Fyfield, returning by the Essex Way long distance footpath by the banks of the river Roding.*

SET OFF TOWARDS ONGAR along the footpath beside the busy A414 passing White Gates to reach The Four Wantz roundabout. Turn right along the B184 Dunmow road passing the BP service station and the Ongar Sale Rooms. At the junction take the pedestrian crossing and enter Moreton Road. Cross to the right-hand side and take the path between numbers 38 and 42.

Beyond the allotments the path passes through bushes before coming out along the right side of a cultivated field. At the point where the field boundary bears right, stop and turn left. Your route is straight across the open field making for the far side and passing to the left of the hedges enclosing a garden which intrudes into the field. (Others appear to have left their mark crossing to the right of the gardens but this is not the correct line). On the far side of the field you should locate a plank bridge in the hedge. Note: if you wish to follow their path - which would indeed be easier going - turn left when you reach the fir trees at the right-hand corner of the garden boundary and follow it past a short section of moat. Then follow the boundary hedge right into the field corner and left for a short distance to locate the stile in the hedge on your right.

Go diagonally left across the meadow and over a footbridge beside a cartbridge spanning the Cripsey Brook. Turn right and follow the left bank, walking roughly parallel with the road. At a post bearing a blue waymark arrow beside a ford, turn half left and head across the meadow away from the Cripsey passing another post, this one bearing a yellow arrow to reach a stile in the hedge and Moreton Road again.

Turn right, soon passing Gothic Cottage. Go over a stile on the right by a single oak tree and take the indistinct path forking left across a small meadow. Cross a stile and plank bridge set in a rustic post and rail fence on your left by the brook and continue by the left bank beside a field. At a point where the brook swings right, you leave it to carry straight on over the field towards a wood, passing under power lines. On the far side continue along the left side of the field with the wood on your left. At the end go over a stepless stile and plank bridge to reach a meadow. Head straight over, passing a seat, and with the buildings of Wood farm over on your left. Cross the raised grass track and look for the step in the post and rail fence enabling you to enter and cross the paddock ahead. Leave by another step in the far fence and pick up the left bank of the brook, again going left and right along a grassy track, then by the right side of a cultivated field following the power lines. When you reach an area of long grass at a point where the brook bears away right, again leave it to carry on ahead still following the power lines, to a telegraph pole bearing a waymark arrow, and a plank bridge. Carry straight on across the next field to pick up an earthen track on the far side. Keep on ahead along the left side of the field. Continue along the right side of the next field until you come to a stile and footbridge on your right where you cross the brook to enter a long meadow. Turn left and head up the meadow passing under the power lines and to the left of the laurel hedge bordering the grounds of Upper Hall. Leave the meadow by a wooden gate and turn right along the road and left up the drive to Moreton Church.

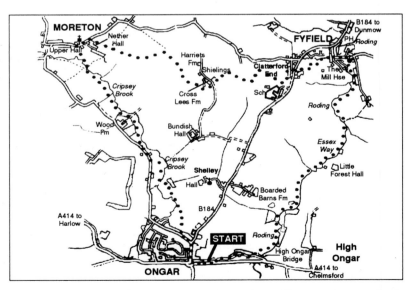

St Mary the Virgin stands on a superb elevated site. The steeple was rebuilt in 1787 by the warden, James King, but the body of the church is old; the nave and chancel are both early 13th century. The interior has a plain, rather puritan charm and a font dating back to c1200.

100

Come back down to the road and turn left passing the entrance to Nether Hall and taking the footpath right, beside a wooden farm gate just before the road bend. Turn left and walk up to locate a wide grassy track going right, parallel with a line of trees and passing between farm buildings and a large liquid storage tank. Join a firm stony track going left and heading away from the farm between open fields. The track heads down the valley and up the far side giving extensive views to the right. When it ends at a cross-track you continue ahead through an open field taking the right fork - if you can see a transformer on a telegraph pole in the distance ahead you are on the right line. At the end of the field turn half right and walk diagonally over the next. At the internal field corner cross a culvert over the ditch and turn left to walk along a wide grassy ride along the left side of a field with a high hedge on your left. Pass a post and rail fence to a paddock on the left and at the end of the field cross an earthen track on a bend and go over the stile ahead, into a grazing meadow enclosed by wire fencing. Turn half left and head over to another stile on the far side passing just to the right of farm buildings. Turn left and go through a single wooden gate by Cross Leas Farm.' Pass the farmhouse and turn immediately right over the concrete yard and between open barns.

Pass to the right of a young oak tree to pick up a rough track. Cross a wide culvert and bear right, walking a rough track between open fields. Cross an opening by a green lane and continue along the left side of the next field. School buildings appear ahead and, at the end of the field, you turn left to walk along the edge of the playing field. Pass a cross-hedge and continue through a rough grass meadow, turning right at the end to follow the boundary hedge. Ignore the path going off left and continue to the end of the meadow, walk on between the hedge and a fence following the power lines down towards the road. When the fence ends carry on ahead through the rough grass. At the ditch go left and right and along the right side of a field. The field boundary swings left and you follow it as it bends left and right to skirt the rear gardens of a line of houses. Look out for a footpath sign directing you right, through a wide gap between houses - often very overgrown - and out to Clutterford End, a cul-de-sac.

This is Fyford. Cross the cul-de-sac and the road beyond with care and enter the driveway to Clutterford Lodge. Walk along the left side of the grounds over the grass and out through a gap into the corner of a field. Turn right and walk along the wide grass ride. Follow the field boundary left and at the end cross a plank bridge across the ditch and set off along the right side of the playing field. About half way along turn half left and head diagonally over to the far corner where you pick up an enclosed path leading you out to the road at a bend. A 150 yards detour left along the road will take you to The Queens Head, but your route is right, crossing the footbridge beside the road bridge over the River Roding.

> The Roding is not naturally a wide river, but at this point it was artificially widened to serve a watermill. The view from the bridge down the river to the converted Mill House is delightful.

A short distance further on you take a firm, wide track on the right just before the church which you may like to visit first.

> The weatherboarded top with octagonal spire gives St Nicholas's a more appealing appearance than perhaps the rather bland and austere body of the church merits, however, the nave and massive crossing tower are Norman with much Roman tile evident and the remainder is mostly 14th century. Part of the tower was rebuilt in brick in the 19th century. Inside is a late 12th century font.

Back on the track pass a cute Gothic-style cottage to reach a metal gate. Enter a meadow and walk along the left side by the rear gardens of properties lining Cannons Lane. Beyond the houses a wide grassy ride, part of a set-aside, bears right, running beside the remaining cultivated field. The ride turns right and you stay with it to the end where you meet the Roding again. Turn left and set off beside the river which you will follow for the next one and a half miles - almost to the end of the walk. At the end of the field cross Tun Bridge, a footbridge, and turn left to pick up a well-worn path now following the right bank. This is part of The Essex Way, a long distance footpath running from Dedham on the Suffolk border to Epping.

You will require few directions from here on; however, one word of warning. On several occasions the path divides at points where the river swings left at field boundaries. One path forks left to stay by the river bank while the other bears right following the field boundary; these divisions are usually accompanied by a footbridge over the dividing ditch but some are partially hidden and not easy to see. In every case bear left with the river path. If you appear to be walking away from the river at any stage you are clearly following a field edge path and not the river path, so retrace your steps.

Your only sign of habitation along the way is Little Forest Hall, while the only feature of note is a long section of woodland which the Roding skirts.

Eventually you enter a meadow and sight High Ongar road bridge ahead. Pass a weir and turn half right to head diagonally over the meadow, away from the river, making for the far right-hand corner by houses. Here a stile beside a metal gate leads you back to High Ongar Road, once the main road but now bypassed by the new stretch of A414 running parallel. Turn right and walk the 600 yards back to your starting point.

The River Stort

THE STORT, known in its infancy as 'Lesser Stour', rises at the point where three counties meet - Essex, Cambridgeshire and Hertfordshire - near to Essex's highest point of 458'.

Its first 12 miles are in Essex after which it forms the county boundary with Hertfordshire. After some 27 miles, just past Harlow, it is joined by the Lea and continues for a further 21 miles, passing through Greater London, to reach the Thames at Barking Creek.

The Lea & Stort Navigation was completed in 1769 and its tow path still runs for some 24 miles from Bishop's Stortford to Waltham Abbey.

The canal, road and railway run side by side between Bishop's Stortford and Harlow, each still actively promoting its own style of transport.

The River Stort at Sheering Mill Lock (Walk 23).

THE RIVER STORT
Walk 23: Little Hallingbury, Harlow
& Sawbridgeworth

Start: *Little Hallingbury is on the A1060 just south of Bishop's Stortford and west of the M11. Take the turning right signposted to Gaston Green and, after a short way, park on the left opposite Little Hallingbury Free Church.*

O.S.Maps: *Landranger 167; Pathfinder 1097.*

Distance: *8½ miles*

Refreshments: *You will pass The White Horse and Riverside Restaurant in Harlow at the halfway stage of the walk, and the Mill & Granary Restaurants at the end.*

Description: *Much of the first half of the walk is quite strenuous, taking you round and over several open cultivated fields but, while you may arrive at Harlow quite exhausted by the effort, don't despair, the return to Little Halling-bury along the river tow path is both delightful and relaxing, alternating between busy, colourful locks and peaceful water meadows.*

YOU BEGIN YOUR WALK along the road, usually quiet, but as there are no footpaths or verges as you head round the left-hand bend, take extra care. Pass the junction with Grinstead Lane and, opposite Little Bursteads, leave the road by turning left to take the path through a field. Pick up a rough grassy bridleway and follow it left at the telegraph pole heading down between open fields in the general direction of the banked M11. At the end of the field the track swings right to fleetingly join the Three Forests Way, a long distance footpath. Continue for some way following the irregular field boundary parallel with the motorway.

At a grassed area by the end of a wood (with another small wood over on your left), leave the Way by turning right at the yellow waymark arrow and head through the light woodland. A rough grass track continues beyond the wood dotted with oaks. At a junction of tracks ignore an arrow directing you right and carry on ahead towards Great Hyde Hall along the right side of a field. At the end bear left and continue to the road where you turn left.

Just before a row of houses on the right, turn right along a concrete drive to Quickbury Farm. Here you leave the drive, passing to the left of the main buildings along the right side of a field. Continue along the field boundary. There are few signs that others have been this way before you but be assured you are on course. As the boundary bears left go over a stile into the meadow on your right and continue as before along the top of the slope (still following the field boundary) as the meadow funnels down to a stile beside a metal gate. Turn right and take a narrow path between cultivated fields, accompanied by the roar from the motor-way just to your left, to reach a metalled lane. Turn left and right along Back Lane to pass above the din to a junction with the B183 at a point where it crosses the M11. Cross over Harlow Road, negotiate a stile and go down the shady path, a haven from the bedlam down below.

Cross a stile at the end and continue along the left side of a field with the panorama of the motorway opening up ahead. You pass a pedestrian footbridge spanning the road and may wish to linger for a few minutes to watch the less fortunate 'pound the tarmac'. Fascinating as it is, don't dally too long as we still have a little way to

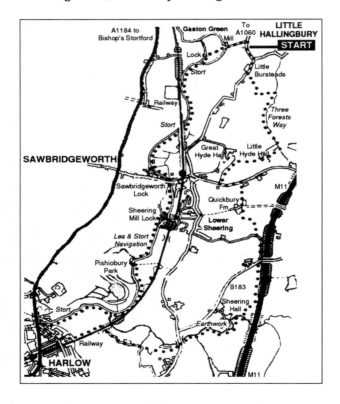

go to the river. Follow the field boundary right, gradually heading back to peace and sanity. Turn left to follow the right side of a field on a grassy track for 100 paces and, when it bears right towards the farm, leave it to carry straight on through the field. On the far side cross a concrete footbridge over a stream and turn right to follow the field boundary and the stream towards Sheering Hall.

You join a concrete track at a point where the stream drops over a small weir and walk along it to a point where it swings left and heads for the motorway. Leave it here, going right with the stream as it skirts the wooded farm boundary. As you walk you should catch glimpses through the trees of ancient bush-covered earthworks which the stream partially encloses and on which I can provide no information. Follow the stream's meandering course and the field edge which turns left and eventually ends at a small copse by the road.

Cross the road and turn left for a few paces before taking the footpath sign beside a cottage. Go over a stile and along the left side of a pasture. Carry straight on, further stiles taking you past a small lake and on out to a lane. Turn right, the metalled lane passing an old bungalow and heading through the trees to become a pleasant shady green lane. Pass under the brick arch of the railway bridge and turn left over a stile and along the left side of a meadow walking parallel with the railway embankment. At the end go over a substantial footbridge and right along a path. Cross an area of rough grass and go left between wooden fences towards the houses on the outskirts of Harlow. Go through a wooden kissing gate and turn right along Wheatfields between houses up to the road and The White Horse.

Turn right to head down Old Road and, just before you reach the main A1184, turn right behind the wooden Riverside Restaurant to reach the tow path of the River Stort just to the right of the road bridge.

This is a good spot for a break before setting off along the tow path which will take you all the way back to Little Hallingbury.

The stream which you followed earlier comes in to join the river at a footbridge and later you pass your first lock, switching to the left bank of the river via a footbridge, and passing Pishiobury Park Visitor Moorings. Rows of gaily-painted barges announce your arrival at Sheering Mill Lock on the Lea & Stort Navigation where you cross the road and carry on past the lock and a row of attractive, modern riverside apartments, well designed along the lines of the old warehousing you pass next, which have now been converted into small business units.

You reach Sawbridgeworth and cross the road, switching back to the right bank and passing Sawbridgeworth Lock. The river heads back out into peaceful countryside and passes under the railway. Cross two small footbridges before the river finally bears right away from the railway and then swings left to reach Little Hallingbury Lock via a footbridge.

Here you leave the river by turning right and crossing the meadow. Go through an opening and cross the next section of meadow on a faint path to reach steps leading up to a footbridge over the mill pool at Little Hallingbury Mill, now a restaurant. Head up the shady Mill Lane to reach the road. A few steps right will return you to your starting point by the Free Church.

Flame streaked clouds pursue the rim of night,
Dappling gold the misty creeks below.
A creeping tide uprights the dinghies' masts,
And caresses the oystercatcher's toes
As they bow their heads to the morning rites,
And lapwings dance on the wildfowler's hide.
Beyond the headland,
The curlew's cry on the rising wind
That parts the quivering reeds
And ruffles the shelduck's back,
Breaks the estuary calm.

('Daybreak over the Mudflats' - Grace Gafney)

Selected Bibliography

The King's England (Essex) - Arthur Mee
Essex - J.Charles Cox
The Buildings of England (Essex) - Nikolaus Pevsner
The Rivers Chelmer & Blackwater - Stan Jarvis
Essex Rivers & Creeks - Robert Simper
Tideways & Byways of Essex & Suffolk - Archie White
Seagates of the Saxon Shore - Kenneth Wenham Strugnell
Rivers of South Essex - Vernon Clarke
Rivers of West Essex - Vernon Clarke
Essex River Colne its Tributaries & Creeks - Vernon Clarke
Battlefields of Britain - David Smurthwaite

The Castell Walking Series

A Walkers' Guide to Suffolk *
A Walkers' Guide to Norfolk *
River & Coastal Walks in Suffolk Vol.I *
River & Coastal Walks in Suffolk Vol.II +
River & Coastal Walks in Essex *
River & Coastal Walks in Norfolk +
Historic Walks in Suffolk +
Historic Walks in Norfolk +
Historic Walks in Essex +

(* *Available 1997*   + *Available 1998/9*)

Notes

Notes

Notes

Notes

Notes

Notes

Notes